CRJ 200 AIRCRAFT SYSTEMS STUDY GUIDE

A Study Guide For The CRJ 200

A Complete Systems Oral Exam Guide for the CRJ 200 Pilot

Aviation Study Made Easy

THIRD EDITION

By Aaron Boone

Boone and Rile Publishing [boonerilepublishing.com] • Peachtree City, GA

CRJ 200 Aircraft Systems Study Guide
By Aaron Boone
www.crjstudyguide.com

Captain Aaron Boone has logged over 7,000 hours in 16 years of flying as a pilot. He holds an ATP, CFI, CFII and MEI pilot certificates. Aaron holds type ratings in the CL-65 Canadair Regional Jet, EMB-120 Brasilia, Citation CE-500, CE-560XL and the King Air BE-300.

© 2010 Boone & Rile Publishing
All rights reserved. Published 2010.

Printed in the USA
ISBN 978-0-9790767-4-9

The purpose of this book is to assist pilots in preparing for a CRJ 200 training event. The user of this information assumes all risk and liability arising from such use. Your company material, procedures, and manuals should be the final authority.

While every attempt is made to ensure that the information in this manual is correct, no liability can be accepted by the author or publisher for loss, damage or injury caused by any errors in, or omissions from, the information given. Please visit our web site www.crjstudyguide.com for updates to this book. We also distribute updates via our newsletter so please sign up.

Self-Publishing & Design Partners: Studio 6 Sense • www.studio6sense.com

Contents

Aviation Study Made Easy

This is the most complete CRJ 200 study guide on the market. This guide is laid out in a question/answer format, containing over 1,200 questions and answers on the CRJ 200 systems that will challenge your brain more than multiple-choice or reading a manual.

Preparing for a checkride by skimming through an aircraft manual is ineffective and unfocused. It is very easy to miss important information, fall asleep, or get side tracked. This study guide has taken all of the important information and put it into a simple question and answer format. Unnecessary information has been left out

The goal of this book is to make your study time more effective so you don't have to spend as much time preparing.

The Aviation Study Made Easy System will allow you to find the specific information you need to work on. After finding these areas, you won't waste a minute going over material you already know. This will help in your recurrent training because you have identified the information that you most easily forget.

You don't need a great memory. What does it take to make good grades in college or smoothly get through the CRJ 200 oral exam? The answer is study habits, study skills, and memory. Sure, some people are smarter than others and have to spend less time studying, but what it comes down to is study habits, study skills, and memory.

Study habits and skills. Let's look at study habits and skills (SHS). If you are learning to fly a CRJ 200, your SHS are probably fairly good. From what I've noticed, though, most pilots still need a little more help. Many pilots spend too much time going over material they already know. When a pilot says, "I'm going to read that chapter again," they are wasting a lot of valuable time going over information they already know. Even if you highlight the important material, you still have to determine if it is information you need to review again, and that takes time, time you may not have to spare.

So how do you quickly eliminate material you already know? Putting all of the information into questions with answers solves this problem. After going through the questions once, you will have marked and eliminated 40-60% of them. The second time through you can focus 100% of your time on the rest of the information. By the time you go through this guide a third time, you can focus 100% of your time on maybe 15% of the information. The amount of information each pilot will eliminate will be different, but the main idea is that no time is spent on information you already know.

If you can eliminate all or most of the questions in this study guide, you will not have a problem with the oral. You can go into the exam with confidence because you have proven to yourself that you can answer all of the questions in this guide. I bet you haven't gone into a checkride with that much confidence before.

Memory. When it comes to memory, some pilots have a better one than others. This means that they have to be exposed to the information less than others to fully retain it. With this study guide, you can focus 100% of your time on the information you don't have in your memory. Sure, it may take you a little more work than the pilot with a better memory, but you are using your time efficiently. In fact, you may be ready for your training event before someone with a better memory if you use this system and they just study by reviewing and re-reading the chapters in their manuals.

This is the system I used in college, and it worked. I was much more organized, and I knew when my studying was done and I was ready for the test. When I then took the test, I usually made an A.

How to best use this book. You need to have 3-4 different colored markers. Go through the book in its entirety. Cover the answer and try to form your own response to the question. If you answer the question correctly, and you don't think you will forget it before your checkride, then mark the question with a particular color. If you did not answer the question correctly, leave it unmarked and go to the next. Do this throughout the entire guide.

When you are done with the first read-through, start over and review only the questions that were not marked. If you answer an unmarked question correctly, and you don't think you will forget it by your checkride, mark the question with a second, different color. Do this over and over. Soon you will only have a few questions that are not marked and these are the ones you are having the most difficulty memorizing or understanding.

You ask, "Why the different color markers?" This will help in later training events because the different colors will identify the questions you had the most difficulty with. You may only need to focus on the questions that took two or three readings.

Depending on your airline training department, some questions may have a very unlikely chance of being asked. If you are sure that your training department will not ask a certain question, mark it with a particular color to identify this. Some training departments want a pilot to know all the details about an aircraft and some do not. I wanted the book to be thorough with all of the systems information so each pilot could decide how to best use the information.

I think you will find the Aviation Study Made Easy System very useful. Training really can be fun, efficient, and less stressful.

Receive your revisions to this book via email.

Please sign up for our newsletter at

www.crjstudyguide.com

Checkride
Tips

Find your pace: During a checkride, pilots usually perform at different speeds, leading to inconsistency and mistakes. Mistakes most likely occur when the pilot speeds up due to the pressure of the situation. Everyone gets nervous before and during a checkride, it is human nature. Controlling this nervousness will help you perform better.

There is really no malfunction or situation in the simulator that requires you to execute a decision and checklist at the speed of light. You can do what is required of you at the same pace you do any normal procedure. Remember, being accurate is much more beneficial than speed. Also, what you feel as slow in an emergency is actually a perfectly acceptable speed.

Handle a malfunction at the same pace as you do anything else while flying the aircraft. Think of the pace at which you execute a normal checklist, perform a normal takeoff, or perform a descent checklist. These are low-pressure situations and you perform these tasks at a nice smooth pace.

An engine failure at V1 can be handled at this same pace. Take a second to think through the malfunction, then react like you where taught to at the pace you do any other checklist.

When you call for or read a checklist, do it at a normal pace similar to speaking or reading. You will find that your thinking is much clearer and more accurate. You may feel like you are going slowly, but this is a good thing.

Almost any problem that occurs in the aircraft there is a profile, a checklist, or is laid out in a procedure exactly how the pilot is to handle it. Just execute it at a smooth pace and you probably won't have a problem.

Think. When you are executing a normal or emergency checklist, think about what you are doing. When a pilot gets comfortable after many hours in the aircraft, it is a tendency to do and say things out of routine or just try to get the checklist done. For example, when the checklist tells you to turn the left main generator off, think before you grab. Some pilots tend to just reach up to the electrical control panel and grab a switch, sometimes it is the wrong switch. Take a second to think before you execute any part of a checklist. You will find that you are a much more accurate pilot. When you think for a second, you will also find that you slow down your pace.

I hope these tips help make your next checkride less stressful and more successful.

chapter 1

Automatic Flight Controls

Your company materials are always the first authority on any information.

What two systems are integrated by the Automatic Flight Control System (AFCS)?

Flight Director and the Autopilot Systems.

What four systems does the AFCS supply information to?

- Dual flight directors

- Two-axis autopilot

- Automatic pitch trim

- Two yaw dampers

What are the four system components of the AFCS?

- Flight control panel (FCP)

- Two flight control computers (FCC)

- Both autopilot servomotors

- Both yaw dampers

What are the main AFCS microprocessors and where are they located?

Flight Control Computers (FCC) 1 and 2. They are located in the IAPS.

What systems do the FCCs provide instructions to?

- FCP

- FDs

- Yaw dampers

- AP servo motors

The flight director receives its position on the primary flight display (PFD) from what system?

The FCCs

What is the IAPS?

The Integrated Avionics Processing System. This system contains many computers and components and provides the means for them to communicate.

Are both FDs always active?

During most modes, one flight director is supplying guidance information to both PFDs. The other FD is in standby but they do continue to continuously cross talk. During the following modes, both FDs are active and providing onside information:

- Takeoff mode

- Approach mode

- Go around mode

What occurs if the active FD fails?

A white FD1 or FD 2 FAIL EICAS status message will be displayed. Also a red FD in a box will appear on the PFDs.

Where are the vertical and lateral mode selections of the FD displayed?

On the Flight Mode Annunciator (FMA) located at the top of the PFDs.

Explain the two fields of the FMA?

A vertical cyan line separates the two fields, with the left side the active field and the right side the armed field. The top line of the FMA displays the active and armed FD lateral mode and the bottom line the active and armed FD vertical mode. The active side is green text and the armed side is white text.

What information do the FCCs process to figure the flight of the aircraft?

The information needed comes from the attitude and heading reference system (AHRS) and the air data computer (ADC).

What happens if information in the FMA field is invalid?

If any information is invalid, it is indicated by a red line where the text would be.

When can only one FD command bar be removed from the PFDs and when will both FD command bars be removed by a selection of the FD button on the FCP?

Selection of the FD FCP button on the side that is not active will remove the FD command bars from that side only. Selection of the FD FCP button on the side that is active will remove both FD command bars.

If the autopilot (AP) is engaged, will deselecting the FD button on the active side disengage the AP?

No, the onside FD button is inactive and deselecting it will not disengage the AP. If the off-side FD button is pressed, the FD bars on the off-side will be removed and will not disengage the AP.

What is the purpose of the XFR button on the FCP?

This button selects the active FD in some modes. It can also be stated that it selects which FCC will command the FDs in some modes. Remember that some modes, the onside FCC will command only the onside FD (Example: APPR mode).

What FD modes are both FDs active and display information received from the onside FCC?

- Takeoff mode (TOTO)

- Approach mode (APPR)

- Go around mode (GAGA)

FCC 1 controls FD1 only and FCC2 controls FD2.

What do the FCC status indicator lights on the flight control panel (FCP) indicate?

When a mode button is selected the request is sent to the FCCs and if the FCCs determine that all conditions are met for that function, the green lights will illuminate. The light to the left of the respective button indicates FCC 1 has acknowledged the request and the light to the right that FCC 2 has acknowledged the request.

What does the flight director synchronization switch (FD SYNC) do when the AP is engaged?

Nothing

What is the purpose of the FD SYNC switch?

When the AP is not engaged, it synchronizes vertical and lateral values at the time of selection.

What happens when the FD SYNC button is pressed and released while the FD has an active vertical mode?

There is a yellow SYNC message in the armed field of the FMA and it will stay there for 3 seconds. The FD is synchronized to the current aircraft vertical mode selected and the FD will maintain this pitch even if the actual aircraft pitch is changed. Ex: If IAS is selected and the FD SYNC is pressed, the FD will match the current pitch to maintain the current IAS.

What happens when the FD SYNC button is pressed and held while the FD has an active vertical mode?

There is a yellow SYNC message in the armed field of the FMA and it will stay there until the SYNC button is released. The FD is synchronized to the current aircraft pitch and bank and it will maintain synchronized even if the aircraft changes it's pitch and bank.

How do you disable the active lateral mode of the FD?

Re-select the active FCP button or select another lateral mode.

What heading will the FD maintained when the TOGA switch is pressed on a go-around?

The FD will hold the heading at the time of activation.

Explain the take-off mode of the FMA when the aircraft is on the ground?

Pressing the TOGA button will display a green "TO" in the vertical and lateral active mode of the FMA. This is achieved by pressing one of the TOGA switches prior to the take-off roll. The lateral mode will hold the heading at weight off wheels. The vertical mode will set the FD command bars at 15 degrees pitch-up when both engines are running.

Pressing the TOGA button will also update the position in the FMS.

What is the default lateral mode of the FD?

Roll mode

If there is not a lateral mode selected at the time the AP is engaged, what lateral mode will the AP maintain?

If the bank angle is less than 5 degrees, the FD will roll level. If the bank angle is greater than 5 degrees, the FD maintains the bank angle at the time of AP engagement.

How can the AP disconnect warning be canceled after the TOGA switch is pressed on a go-around?

Push the TOGA switch again or push the AP disconnect switch on the control wheel.

What occurs to the FD lateral mode if the navigation source is lost?

Reverts to roll mode.

How are lateral FD modes selected?

The lateral FD modes are activated or armed by buttons on the FCP or the TOGA switches on the thrust levers.

When the localizer captures, what FCP modes will automatically clear if engaged?

It clears the heading mode, half bank, and the turbulence mode.

What course must be set when using the back course mode?

The front course must be set.

How is the go-around mode indicated on the FMA?

The lateral and vertical mode on the active FMA has the green text GA.

Explain the half bank option of the FD?

This button will restrict the FD bank to 15 degrees. It is automatically selected climbing through 31,600 feet and automatically turned off descending through 31,600 feet.

It is not available during a go-around mode, takeoff mode, on-side localizer or approach capture.

How is an active vertical mode disabled?

Select another vertical mode, or re-select the active FCP button.

What are the ways to arm or activate a vertical mode?

- The vertical mode buttons like VS on the FCP or the pitch wheel on the FCP. If just the pitch wheel is rotated after a new altitude is selected, pitch mode will be activated.

- TOGA switches.

How is a pre-selected altitude armed when set in the altitude alerter?

When a vertical mode is selected like VS or IAS.

How is the altitude capturing point of the FD determined?

It is determined by the closure rate. With high vertical speeds the capture point is further from the altitude.

If the vertical speed of the aircraft is only 500 fpm, then altitude capturing occurs within about 50 feet of the selected altitude. When the vertical speed is 3,000 fpm, then altitude capture can occur even before the 1,000 feet to level off occurs.

Explain the altitude capture process in the FMA?

With a new altitude selected there is a white ALTS in the vertical armed portion of the FMA. When the ALTS mode is captured, the white ALTS disappears and a green ALTS CAP appears in the active vertical portion of the FMA and will flash for 5 seconds and then become steady.

The altitude capture will continue until the aircraft is within 100 feet of the pre-selected altitude. At this point, the ALTS CAP message is replaced with a green flashing ALTS that will also flash for 5 seconds and then becomes steady. The FD is now holding the selected altitude.

How is the Altitude Alerting System (ALS) connected to the FD and AP systems?

The ALS is independent of the FD and AP system. It processes information from the air data computers (ADC).

During a climb or descent, when will the ALS alert of the impending level off?

1,000 feet prior to the pre-selected altitude.

How does the ALS alert of an impending level off?

An aural tone and a flashing ALTS on the FMA.

If the FD is tracking an altitude, what warnings will be given if there is an altitude deviation?

If the aircraft deviates by more than 100 feet from the selected altitude, the altitude bugs flash and there will be a series of tones.

If the deviation continues, at 1,000 feet from the selected altitude, there will be an aural tone and the altitude bugs and digital readout flash amber.

What are the ten vertical FD modes?

1. Pre-select altitude (ALTS)

2. Pitch (PTCH)

3. Takeoff (TO)

4. Go-around (GA)

5. Vertical approach mode (GS)

6. Vertical speed (VS)

7. Speed (IAS)

8. Descent (DES)

9. Climb (CLB)

10. Altitude hold (ALT)

When the FD is in the vertical takeoff mode, what will the FD pitch to if there is an engine failure?

It will change pitch from 15 degrees to 10 degrees.

How can the pitch mode of the FD be activated?

If no vertical mode is selected and the AP is engaged the FD will default to pitch mode. Pitch mode can be engaged by a third press of the SPEED button or by rotating the pitch trim wheel on the FCP with a vertical mode other than VS selected.

If an altitude is captured, a new altitude must be selected to activate a vertical mode.

If the aircraft is climbing or descending and the ALT button on the FCP is pressed, what altitude will the FD maintain?

The FD will level and then climb or descend to capture the pressure altitude at the time the ALT mode button was pressed.

What must be done before SPEED mode can be engaged?

A new altitude must be selected in the altitude selector.

How will a speed mode be displayed on the FMA?

Speed mode will be displayed as CLB, DES, IAS or MACH on the FMA. When a speed mode is active an ALTS will be in the vertical armed field of the FMA.

When selecting SPEED mode, how do you select whether the aircraft will climb or descend?

A new pre-selected altitude must be set. Climb or descend depends if the selected altitude is above or below actual altitude.

Explain the difference between a green CLB 250 and an IAS 250 in the active FMA on the PFD.

CLB ### is activated by pressing the SPEED button on the FCP once with a pre-selected altitude set that is above the current altitude. If the target airspeed is increased the FCC will direct the FD to pitch down but never lower than 50 feet per minute (fpm) and then climb once the airspeed is achieved.

IAS ### is activated by a second press of the SPEED button, and the aircraft will maintain the selected airspeed even if it means going from a climb to a descent.

Note: Vertical DES and vertical IAS mode are the same.

What would occur if the SPEED button were pressed consecutively?

The vertical modes will cycle between CLB or DES, IAS and PTCH.

How is IAS ### on the active FMA activated?

By pressing the SPEED button on the FCP twice.

Explain the vertical IAS mode?

A second press of the SPEED button on the FCP activates this mode. A new pre-selected altitude must be selected for the aircraft to leave the altitude hold. If a climb or descent is desired, the thrust levers are increased or decreased and the speed will be maintained.

The aircraft will go in the opposite direction of the desired altitude to achieve the target speed. Example: If the selected IAS is higher than the current speed, the FD could command a descent to achieve the target airspeed.

At what altitude is there an automatic change over from indicated airspeed to Mach in the FMA?

The change over occurs at 31,600 feet.

How do you manually change from IAS to Mach on the FMA?

By pressing the center of the SPEED selection knob.

Each click of the pitch trim wheel on the FCP is equal to how many feet?

100 feet

When the TOGA switch is pressed during a go-around, how many degrees pitch-up will the FD command bars indicate?

10 degrees

The TOGA switch is pressed on a go-around, how can the autopilot warning be cancelled?

By pushing the AP disconnect switch on the control wheel or a second press of the TOGA switch.

What control surfaces do the AP servos provide command inputs to?

Only the elevators and ailerons. The rudder is controlled by the yaw damper system.

What conditions must exist for the autopilot to be engaged with the selection of the AP ENG button on the FCP?

- No significant instability of the aircraft exists.

- Both FCCs are working.

- At least one yaw damper is engaged.

- Minimum of one channel of the horizontal stabilizer is

engaged and the FCCs determine that there are no faults with the horizontal stabilizer pitch system.

When the AP is engaged, what is the indication of a control surface being significantly out-of- trim?

There is an amber EICAS message indicating whether it is the aileron or the elevator and in what direction. There will also be an amber-boxed E or A on the PFDs.

Caution Msg: AP Trim is LWD or RWD and AP Trim is ND or NU.

Where is the activation of the TURB mode indicated on the PFD?

There is nothing on the PFD to indicate that the TURB mode is engaged. The only indication is the two green lights on the sides of the TURB button. The lights indicate that the left and right FCCs respectively approve the selection of this mode.

What automatically clears the TURB mode?

A localizer capture.

What are the aural and visual indications that the autopilot has been disengaged?

There is a red flashing AP→ on the PFD and the autopilot aural warning sounds for approximately 5 seconds.

What are the ways the autopilot can be manually disengaged and what warning will be given?

- Pressing the YD DISC pushbutton, which will disconnect both YDs.

- Pressing either TOGA switch.

- Pressing the AP ENG pushbutton.

- The AP DISC on the FCP.

- The stab trim split switches on the control wheel.

- Either AP/SP DISC button on the control wheels.

There will be the aural warning sound for approximately 5 seconds and the red flashing AP→ on the PFD.

If the autopilot system has a fault that causes the autopilot to disengage, will the warning be the same as when the autopilot is manually disconnected?

Same indications but either AP/SP DISC switch must be pressed to cancel the flashing AP→ on the PFD and the aural warning.

What conditions will cause the autopilot to automatically disengage?

- Wind shear.

- Stall warning.

- Failure of both YDs.

- During wind shear avoidance procedures.

- During unusual attitudes.

Is the FD sync usable with the autopilot engaged?

No

What is the purpose of the button in the center of the course knob?

Centers the HSI needle to the VOR station if it is being received.

If a new FD mode is selected and becomes active, what is the annunciation in the FMA?

For 5 seconds it will flash green and then go steady.

What is happening when the AP XFR button on the FCP is activated?

The co-pilots FCC gives guidance to both FDs. The exception to this is during APPR, TO and GA modes when the FCC 1 and 2 are providing onside guidance.

Auxiliary Power Unit

CRJ200

chapter 2

What is the primary and secondary function of the APU?

The primary function of the APU is to operate the accessory gearbox mounted 30 KVA generator. The APU's secondary function is to supply bleed air for air conditioning and engine starting.

What is the maximum operating altitude of the APU?

37,000 feet

Does the APU vary its RPM?

The APU is required to run at a constant 12,000 rpm to maintain a frequency of 400Hz.

Where is the APU located?

The APU is located in the aft equipment bay inside a fireproof titanium enclosure.

What controls and monitors all APU operations?

An automatic electronic control unit (ECU) controls all of the APU operations.

Is the APU ECU DC or AC powered?

The ECU is DC powered.

What is the maximum altitude to start the APU?

30,000 feet

What is the maximum altitude to use APU bleed air?

15,000 feet

What is the maximum altitude to start an engine with the APU?

13,000 feet

How is the flow of air through the compressor controlled?

The air is controlled by the variable geometry diffuser (VGD).

What is the function of the APU VGD?

The VGD helps to protect against surge and stalls and regulates the discharge airflow from the compressor impeller. The VGD opens as the air needed increases during electrical and bleed air loading.

What accessories are mounted on the APU gearbox?

The AC generator, fuel control unit (FCU), oil cooling fan, DC electric starter, and oil pump.

Where is the APU air intake located?

The intake is located on the upper left rear side of the fuselage.

How many positions does the APU intake door have?

It has three positions, open, mid, or closed.

What factors determine the position of the APU intake door?

The position is determined by the ECU and is based on aircraft altitude and true airspeed.

What can be done if the APU door actuator fails and the door is not operable?

Maintenance can mechanically position the door to any of the three positions. This allows the aircraft to be dispatched.

Limitations are that the APU must be operating or if not operating the airspeed is limited to 300 KIAS.

What is the limitation if the APU intake door is failed open or if the door position is unknown?

The airspeed is restricted to 300 KIAS or the APU must remain running then there will not be a restriction.

How many feet is the APU exhaust danger area?

15 feet

How is the APU lubricated?

The APU has a self-contained lubrication system. There is a gearbox mounted oil pump, oil cooler assembly, and an integral oil tank.

What is the purpose of the screened duct on the left rear fuselage?

Air is drawn in through the screen by an APU gearbox driven fan to provide APU oil cooling and ventilation of the APU enclosure.

Where does the APU normally receive fuel?

The APU receives fuel from both wing tanks by the APU/XFLOW pump.

How many pounds an hour does the APU burn?

Approximately 120 pounds an hour with electrical and bleed air loading.

What is the purpose of the XFLOW/APU pump in the operation of the APU?

This pump draws fuel from both wing tanks and sends the fuel to the APU.

How will the APU receive fuel should the XFLOW/APU pump fail?

The APU will receive fuel via the APU negative gravity relief valve, which is pressurized by the right engine fuel feed manifold.

What is the purpose of the APU fuel feed shutoff valve (SOV)?

It is used to control the fuel supply to the APU.

How is the APU SOV opened?

By pressing the PWR FUEL switch light on the APU control panel.

When will the APU SOV close?

It will close manually by pressing the PWR FUEL or the APU FIRE PUSH switch light. It will close automatically when an APU fire is detected.

Which APU SOV is not on the fuel status page?

The fuel solenoid SOV that is located between the APU FCU and the fuel nozzles.

How is the APU fuel solenoid SOV opened?

The APU ECU at 4% rpm opens it.

Once the APU is stabilized, what will influence the fuel scheduling?

EGT, RPM, generator and bleed air demands.

How is the APU shut down normally?

By pressing the APU START/STOP switch light there is a simulated over speed signal generated to close the fuel solenoid SOV. This will stop the flow of fuel and the APU will shut down.

Is the APU fuel solenoid SOV DC or AC powered?

It is DC powered.

When the APU PWR fuel switch light is pressed, what is occurring?

It initiates the APU pre-start sequence.

- The APU IN BITE status message appears on the status page for 5 seconds and then disappears which means it is performing a self-test.

- The RPM AND EGT gauges for the APU are displayed on the status page.

- The APU intake door opens and the door status appears on the status page.

- The APU fuel shutoff valve is opened. The APU SOV OPEN status message appears.

- The XFLOW/APU fuel pump starts.

What happens when the start/stop switch light is pressed during the APU start process?

The ECU will perform the following:

- The APU START status message appears on the status page and the START light in the switch light illuminates. The starter motor is energized.

29

- At 4% rpm fuel and ignition is introduced. Fuel is introduced by the fuel solenoid SOV.

- The starter motor is de-energized by the ECU at 50% rpm, and the START in the switch light extinguishes.

- The green AVAIL light in the START/STOP switch light illuminates at 99% rpm plus 4 seconds. The APU LCV OPEN status message appears.

What does the green AVAIL in the APU START/STOP switch light indicate?

The light means that the APU is ready to accept bleed air loading. This light will come on 4 seconds after the rpm is at 99% or more.

What does the amber PUMP FAIL in the APU PWR FUEL switch light indicate?

It indicates a failed XFLOW/APU pump.

When will the APU starter disengage?

At 50% or when starter engagement time exceeds 60 seconds.

What are the APU start limitations?

APU BATTERY START		
Start	Max Time On	Followed By
1	30 - Seconds	---
2	30 - Seconds	20 - Minutes off
3	30 - Seconds	---
4	30 - Seconds	40 - Minutes off

APU START USING DC GROUND POWER		
Start	Max Time On	Followed By
1	15 - Seconds	---
2	15 - Seconds	20 - Minutes off
3	15 - Seconds	---
4	15 - Seconds	40 - Minutes off

How many igniter plugs does the APU ignition system have?

It has two air-gap igniter plugs.

During the APU start sequence, when is the ignition de-energized?

The ignition is de-energized at 95% rpm.

Which battery is used for starting the APU?

Both the main and APU batteries are required to start and operate the APU. The APU battery is used to turn the APU starter and the main battery is used to operate the APU ECU.

What is the minimum battery voltage to start the APU?

22 volts on both the main and APU battery.

Why do the APU PWR fuel switch light and the APU start/stop switch light have to be pressed within 5 seconds of each other while in flight?

The APU door will open and if the APU is wind milling at a speed greater than 8% rpm before pressing the START switch light, the APU starter will not engage. This is due to the APU ECU inhibit logic.

How long after the APU is stopped can it be restarted?

When the APU is stopped, the ECU initiates a 60-second BITE test. This test must be complete before the APU can be started again.

After the APU is stopped by the START/STOP switch light, when can the PWR/FUEL switch light be deselected?

When the AVAIL light in the START/STOP switch light extinguishes. A better practice is to wait until 10% RPM.

What is the recommended time between cranking attempts of the APU?

Two minutes because this allows the ECU to reset.

Under what conditions will the APU automatically shutdown on the ground and in flight?

Shutdown Conditions	GRD	FLT
Fire: APU fire detected	Y	Y
Slow start: engaged more than 60 seconds	Y	Y
Over speed: RPM greater than 107%	Y	Y
DC power loss	Y	Y
RPM signal lost	Y	Y
EGT signal lost	Y	Note 1,2
ECU Failure: subsystem fault detected or loss of DC power	Y	Y
Low oil pressure	Y	Note 2
High oil temperature	Y	Note 2
EGT over temperature > 743C, EGT >974C and <50% rpm	Y	Note 2
Intake Door position signal lost	Y	Note 2
An electrical short detected on a circuit, over current	Y	Note 2

Note 1: APU bleed air is not available in flight when the EGT signal is lost.
Note 2: The APU control logic reverts to the ground mode 60-seconds after landing.

Explain the APU variable geometry diffuser (VGD).

The VGD is used to protect the compressor from surging or stalling and is controlled by the APU ECU. The vanes, which are located at the compressor discharge, are opened to increase the flow of air through the compressor and closed to decrease the compressor airflow. The need for different airflow amounts is due to electrical and bleed air loading of the APU.

What switch allows bleed air to be supplied to the 10th stage bleed air manifold by the APU?

The APU LCV switch light located on the BLEED AIR control panel.

What is the primary function of the APU?

The APU's primary function is operation of the AC generator and has priority over the bleed air service. The APU LCV will modulate towards closed to reduce the amount of air bled from the APU compressor during combined APU generator and APU bleed air loading.

Explain the two levels of APU compressor stall and surge protection?

- The engines can provide 10th stage bleed air at a much greater pressure that the APU. An APU compressor stall or surge could happen if this high-pressure engine air were to reverse-flow to the APU. To solve this problem, a check valve is installed in the APU bleed air duct to prevent the reverse flow.

- The APU LCV has an interlock function with the 10th stage bleed air switches. If the left 10th stage bleed switch is selected open, the APU LCV will close. If the right 10th stage bleed switch and the isolation valve switches were selected open, the APU LCV will close. It is all tied to switch position.

Can the APU be shutdown from outside the aircraft?

There is a remote cut-off switch located at the external services panel and in the aft equipment bay on the APU.

If the APU is shut down on the ground, what will alert ground personnel?

A warning horn will alert ground personal.

If the APU door position is unknown by the APU ECU, what will indicate this?

The EICAS will show a white DOOR message with amber ---.

What are the APU RPM ranges?

- Green 0 – 100%.

- Amber 101 – 106%.

- Red 107% and above, which will cause an automatic shutdown.

What are the APU EGT ranges?

- Green 0 – 712 C.

- Amber 713 – 742 C.

- Red 743 C or greater or 974 C <50% during start.

chapter 3

Communications

How do you adjust the volume of the aural warning system?

It is not adjustable by the pilots because the aural warning system does not go through the volume control switches.

With the radio transmit (R/T) - intercom (I/C) switch in the I/C position, where can your intercom transmission be heard?

At all interior and exterior interphone units.

What is the purpose of the VOICE/BOTH switch?

BOTH allows the pilot to hear the Morse code and voice messages from the station. VOICE filters out the Morse code so only the voice message can be heard.

Where is the observer overhead speaker located?

The observer seat does not have a speaker; therefore the observers audio control panel speaker knob is inoperative.

Explain the EMER/NORM switch on the ACPs.

When there is a failure of the audio integrating system, the EMER position should be selected. This causes the electronic circuits of the audio integrating system to be bypassed and most of the ACP functions will be inoperative. If the pilot were to select EMER, his headset will be directly connected to NAV 1 and VHF 1. The aural warning system will be operable.

If the co-pilot selects EMER, his headset is connected directly to NAV 2 and VHF 2. All ACP services are lost except for NAV 2 and VHF 2.

The switch on the observer's ACP is disabled.

Explain the public address system (PA) priority.

1. Pilots

2. FA

Pilots can override the FAs PA.

How do you adjust the speaker volume in the cabin, lavatory and galley?

It is adjusted automatically based on the background noise. It is at full volume when the APU or an engine is running.

What would you do if the FA told you that the speaker in the galley was not working when she made her PA?

The galley speaker does not work when PA's are made from the FA's station.

Explain the interphone control unit.

The interphone control unit is located on the center pedestal and has four switch lights: PA, CHIME, CALL, and EMERG. Only one mode can be selected at one time.

How would you make a PA to the cabin?

The ACP transmit switch should be selected to PA, then press the PA switch light. Either the R/T switch on the control wheel, the ACP R/T switch or the handheld microphone can be used to make the PA.

When finished, move the ACP switch from PA to another position will turn it off.

What occurs when the CALL switch light is pressed?

The switch light illuminates green and there is an aural high-low chime. A red light illuminates on the overhead exit sign in the middle of the cabin and the FLT light illuminates green on the FA's handset cradle.

Explain the EMER switch light on the interphone control unit.

It is used to notify the FA of an emergency condition. When pressed the switch light flashes amber and there is an aural high-low chime. There will be a red flashing light on the mid-cabin overhead exit sign and the amber EMG light flashes on the FA's handset cradle.

When the FA calls the flight deck, what should be selected to activate communications?

Select PA on the ACP mic selector switch.

At what locations can maintenance use the interphone system to talk with the pilots?

- Avionics bay

- Aft equipment bay

- Refuel/defuel control panel

- External service panel

Explain the MECH PUSH switch light.

This is a call function between the flight deck and the external service panel and the aft equipment bay. There is a switch light on the three panels will illuminate when one switch is pressed. It will be accompanied with an aural two-tone in the cabin. The lights remain on for 30 seconds.

What is the purpose of the backup tuning unit?

This radio provides control of COM 1 and NAV 1 in the event of complete loss of AC power or both radio-tuning units (RTU) fail. COM 1, NAV 1 and the backup-tuning unit are powered from the battery bus.

What system controls are available on the RTUs?

- VHF communication radios

- VHF navigation radios

- TCAS

- Transponders

- ADF

- Optional HF radio

Explain the two pages of the RTUs.

The RTU has a top page and a main page. The top page allows basic changes to the VHF radios, transponder, ADF and the main page is dedicated to a specific navigation, TCAS or communication system. Pressing the associated button twice activates Main page.

Example: Press the RTU TCAS button twice to access the TCAS main page.

Explain the 1/2 button on the RTU.

This button is the RTU cross-side tuning button. The RTUs are normally set up for on-side control of the radios. The 1/2 key allows one RTU to display and control the other side.

Cross-side information is in yellow. Pushing the 1/2 key a second time will return the radio to a normal on-side display. This feature is used when an RTU fails but the radio and navigation functions still work.

What would you do if your RTU fails and what would it look like?

The display would be blank and cross-side tuning would be inoperative. Cross side tuning needs to be established and inhibiting the failed RTU can do this. This is accomplished by selecting the RTU INHIBIT switch for the failed RTU. Cross-side tuning is now available and can be activated by pressing the 1/2 on the serviceable RTU.

Both radios are available but cannot be shown on one RTU at the same time. The 1/2 button achieves switching between the two radios.

Explain the STBY position of the backup tuning unit.

In this position the backup tuning unit is in standby. The frequencies will duplicate COM 1 and NAV 1 frequencies.

When would you use the backup tuning unit?

When both RTUs and the FMS fail or there is a complete loss of AC power.

Besides the RTUs and the backup tuning unit, where can the radio frequencies be changed?

On the FMS radio tuning page.

Explain the FMS TUNE INHIBIT switch.

When in the INHIBIT position, the remote tuning function of the FMS is inhibited. This may be needed if the remote FMS control malfunctions.

Where is the Cockpit Voice Recorder (CVR) located?

The CVR is located in the tail section of the airplane.

What four locations are recorded on the CVR?

- Pilot station.

- Copilot station.

- Area microphone in the cockpit.

- Mixed PA audio and the observer station.

How long does the CVR record?

There are two types, 30 and 120 minutes. At the end of the cycle it will re-record.

When does the CVR start recording?

When electrical power is applied to the aircraft.

Explain the CVR test button.

When pressed it completes an internal test of the CVR system. To test; hold the button for 5 seconds and a successful test is indicated by illumination of the green light in the button during the 5 seconds.

What is the function of the headset jack on the CVR control panel?

To monitor the recording tone during the test.

Where is the flight data recorder unit (FDR) located?

The FDR is located in the tail section of the aircraft.

What does the FDR record and for how many hours?

It records the last 25 hours of aircraft and flight parameter data.

When does the FDR start recording?

When one of the following three occurs:

- Beacon is ON

- Strobes are ON

- Weight off wheels

What is the purpose of the FDR EVENT switch?

This will highlight an event on the FDR. The highlight is accomplished by pressing the FDR EVENT switch for 2 seconds, which will then display a green FDR EVENT advisory status message.

chapter 4

Doors

What doors are available for emergency evacuation on the ground?

- Passenger door.

- Service door.

- Left and right over wing emergency exit.

- Overhead escape hatch in the cockpit.

The proximity sensing electronic unit (PSEU) monitors which doors?

All except the overhead escape hatch in the cockpit and the aft equipment bay door.

What is the max door load?

The max door load is 1,000 lbs. or 4 passengers on the door at any one time.

What secures the main cabin door?

- Pre-Phase IV: There are three door lock pins on each side of the door and two upper cam latches.

- Phase IV: This door has two pins per side.

What are the indications that the main cabin door is locked?

Pre-Phase IV: There are six green alignment marks on the inside of the door to indicate the pins are in the correct position and there are green alignment marks for the two upper cam latches. When the handle is properly stowed, a green locked/unlocked indicator will indicate locked.

Phase IV: The new door has two pins on each side of the door and two locking cams. The door is verified locked by proper alignment of these pins and cams.

What doors are plug type doors?

- Galley

- Cockpit escape hatch

- Avionics bay

- Over wing emergency exits

- Cargo

How do you confirm the galley door is closed?

A green indicator below the inside handle.

Where is the avionics bay door?

The avionics bay door is on the bottom of the forward fuselage.

Does the PSEU monitor the fore and aft lock pins in the avionics bay door?

The PSEU monitors the forward pin and the handle. Either will give a door open message on the EICAS.

Is the aft equipment bay pressurized?

No

Can the overhead escape hatch be opened from the outside?
Yes

What indicates the overhead escape latch is properly secured?
The two green indicator pins will indicate locked. The pins should align with alignment marks when it is secure.

The over wing emergency exits look identical, can they be switched?
No

Can the over wing exits be opened from the outside?
Yes

What does the EICAS message PASSENGER DOOR indicate?
The passenger door is unsafe and not completely locked and secured.

chapter 5

Electrical System

What is the voltage of the AC and DC system?

The voltage is 115-volt AC and 28-volt DC electrical power.

What are the sources of AC electrical power for the aircraft?

- The primary sources of AC electrical power are two engine driven integrated drive generators (IDGs).

- The APU has an AC generator mounted on it.

- An air driven generator (ADG) can provide AC power if there is a total loss of AC power.

- On the forward right side of the fuselage there is a receptacle for AC ground power.

What provides power if there is a total loss of AC electrical power in flight?

From the right side of the forward fuselage an air driven generator (ADG) is deployed to provide AC power.

What are the sources of DC electrical power?

- Five transformer rectifier units (TRUs)

- Two nickel cadmium (nicad) batteries

- 28-volt external power

How many circuit breaker (CB) panels are there and where are they located?

There are six CB panels, four on the flight deck, one in the aft equipment bay and one at the FA's station.

What is the kilo volt-amperes (KVA) rating of the integrated drive generators (IDG)?

The IDG rating is 30 KVA up to 35,000 feet, then 25 KVA to 41,000 feet.

What type of power do the IDGs supply?

The IDGs supply 115-volt AC, 400-hertz 3-phase electrical power.

Does the IDG RPM vary with engine RPM?

No, the generator must turn at a constant RPM to produce a steady 400-Hz. The constant speed drive (CSD) unit accomplishes this task.

How does the CSD accomplish a constant RPM?

The CSD is a hydro-mechanical unit and uses an integral oil system to drive the generator at a constant RPM. The CSD is driven by the engine accessory gearbox, which turns at a variable speed based on engine speed.

How is the internal oil of the CSD cooled?

The oil in the CSD is cooled by an air/oil heat exchanger. The air used to cool the oil is from the N1 fan.

What does the FAULT light in the IDG switch light indicate?

This light will illuminate when the IDG oil overheats or oil pressure drops below limits. This FAULT light will also illuminate an IDG caution message on the EICAS.

What are the ways that the IDG can disconnect from the engine gearbox?

- By pressing the associated IDG DISC switch.

- When CSD internal temperature raises to a certain temperature the IDG will disconnect.

- An over torque condition of the CSD will cause the shearing of the IDG drive shaft.

What monitors the generator system?

Each generator has a generator control unit (GCU) that controls and monitors the related generator system. The GCU provides protection and voltage regulation for the associated generator.

When will the engine generator automatically be tripped off line and removed from the bus system?

When any of the following occur:

- Generator or bus over current

- Over or under frequency

- Over or under voltage

What is the output of the APU generator?

115 volt AC 400 Hz, and 30 KVA from SL to 37,000 feet.

Where is the external AC receptacle located?

Forward right side of the fuselage.

What does the green AVAIL light on the flight deck electrical power services control panel and the external service panel indicate?

When external AC power is attached to the aircraft, the external monitor checks the AC ground power for proper voltage, frequency, and phase relationship. If it is good power and available for use these AVAIL lights will illuminate.

What occurs when the AC switch light on the flight deck electrical power services panel has the green AVAIL light illuminated and is pressed?

If there is no other AC electrical power available, the external AC power will supply power. The white IN USE of the switch light will illuminate and the green AVAIL will extinguish.

There is external AC power supplying the aircraft power, what will happen if an engine generator is selected on?

The buses will be supplied AC power from the engine generator and no longer from the AC external power. The green AVAIL lamp on the electrical control panel will illuminate and the white IN USE extinguish, even if the switch light is still selected in.

What buses are powered when external AC power is connected and the green AVAIL switch light on the external services panel is pressed?

The utility and services buses will be powered.

How many AC buses does the electrical system have?

6

What is the purpose of the bus priority system?

It is the automatic fault protection and transfer system of the AC electrical system. AC BUS 1 and 2 are important buses and the bus priority ensures that these buses will be powered.

Example: Generator 1 normally powers AC BUS 1. If there is a fault in generator 1, AC BUS 1 will then transfer to the APU generator. If the APU is not available, it will transfer to generator 2. If generator 2 is not available it will look for external power.

What happens when AC BUS 1 has a short and takes generator 1 off line?

The bus priority system will have AC BUS 1 try to receive power from the APU generator, generator 2, then external power in that order. This could take all the generators off line. The auto transfer inhibit will stop the transfer and a amber FAIL light in the AUTO XFER switch will illuminate. The FAIL means if has done its job. FAIL really means auto transfer inhibit of priority logic.

What are the six AC buses?

1. AC BUS 1 (main bus)

2. AC BUS 2 (main bus)

3. AC ESS (Essential) BUS

4. AC SERV (Service) BUS

5. AC UTIL (Utility) BUS 1

6. AC UTIL (Utility) BUS 2

Where in the aircraft are AC BUS 1 and AC bus 2 located?

AC bus 1 is behind the captain's seat on circuit breaker panel 1 and AC BUS 2 is located behind the co-pilot's seat on circuit breaker panel 2.

What other buses do AC BUS 1 supply power to?

Normally to the AC ESS BUS and AC UTIL BUS 1.

Which other buses does AC BUS 2 supply power to?

Normally to AC SERV BUS and AC UTIL BUS 2.

What is the bus priority for AC BUS 1?

1. GEN 1

2. APU generator

3. GEN 2

4. External power

What is the bus priority for AC BUS 2?

1. GEN 2

2. APU generator

3. GEN 1

4. External power

What does the AC ESS BUS power?

It powers equipment essential for flight and powers ESS TRU 1.

What bus normally powers the AC ESS BUS?

AC BUS 1 normally powers the AC ESS BUS. If there were a failure of AC BUS 1, the ESS BUS would sense this and automatically transfer to AC BUS 2 for its power source.

If AC BUS 1 fails, what would you do if the ESS BUS did not automatically transfer to AC BUS 2?

The ESS BUS could be manually transferred to AC BUS 2 by the AC ESS XFER switch light on the electrical power services panel. This will cause the AC ESS XFER switch light to illuminate white and there will be a white status message AC ESS ALTN on the status page. This electrically connects the ESS BUS to AC BUS 2.

What would occur to the AC ESS BUS if total AC power were lost in flight?

The air driven generator (ADG) would automatically deploy and the AC ESS BUS would be powered. The ADG BUS is powered by the ADG and this bus is connected to the AC ESS BUS.

Aircraft generator power is re-established after a total AC power loss and ADG deployment. Will the aircraft generator now power the AC ESS BUS?

To de-energize the relay between the AC ESS BUS and the ADG BUS, the PWR TXFR OVERRIDE button on the ADG AUTO DEPLOY CONTROL panel must be pressed. This will connect the AC ESS BUS to AC BUS 1.

What bus powers the AC SERVICE BUS?

The AC BUS 2 supplies 115-volts AC to the AC service bus.

What does the AC SERVICE BUS power?

This bus provides power to the service outlets that are used for lavatory and cabin cleaning. The AC SERVICE BUS also powers the service TRU that powers the DC SERVICE BUS.

The cleaning crew needs to clean the aircraft, how would you power only the buses needed for cleaning?

- External power available: If the AVAIL lamp in the EXT AC PUSH switch light on the external services panel is illuminated, the switch light could be pressed and if no other AC power were available to the aircraft, the AC SERVICE BUS and AC UTIL 1 and 2 buses would be powered. No other buses would be powered.

- APU is operating: If the APU is operating and the APU generator is selected off, selecting the APU SERVICE BUS switch light at the flight attendant station will energize the service configuration, which are the AC SERVICE BUS and AC UTIL 1 and 2. Note: Before using this option, refer to the AFM for limitations?

Where do the AC UTIL BUS 1 and 2 receive their power and what do they power?

They receive power from AC BUS 1 and 2 respectively. The AC UTIL Bus 1 and 2 provide power to the battery chargers and galley.

Explain the shedding of the utility buses?

During flight and single generator operation occurs, the utility buses will be automatically shed. This will reduce the electrical loading of the single generator.

The utility buses will also be shed during ground operations with a single generator providing power, the flaps are not up, and the main door and service door are closed. Any two generators (including APU) on line will allow the utility buses to be powered.

During single engine taxing with the APU generator operating and flaps not at 0 degrees, are the utility buses shed?

No, with any two generators on line the utility buses will not be shed.

When the aircraft is in the service configuration, what else is being powered besides UTIL BUS 1 and 2?

The battery chargers are powered so the batteries can be charged.

What are the volts, Hz and KVA provided by the ADG?

The ADG provides 115 volts, 400 Hz, 15 KVA.

What part of the electrical system does the ADG power?

The ADG powers the essential buses in flight, but only when all other AC generators are not providing AC power.

The ADG powers the AC ESS Bus, which powers the ESS TRU 1. The ESS TRU 1 powers the DC ESS Bus and the BATT Bus.

Where is the ADG located?

The ADG is located next to the nose gear on the forward right fuselage.

After deployment of the ADG in flight, how can it be retracted?

It can only be retracted on the ground by maintenance.

What are the general components of the ADG?

It has an AC generator and a variable pitch two-bladed propeller.

What are the two types of ADGs installed in the CRJ?

There is a wet and dry model. The wet is the older model and the constant speed of the generator is maintained by controlling propeller pitch angle hydraulically. The dry ADG is the latest model and the constant speed of the generator is maintained by a counterweight to control the propeller pitch.

What are the airspeed limitations of the ADG?

There are none for the dry model.

For the wet: Maximum continuous airspeed is 250 KIAS. Up to 330 KIAS for 12 minutes and 331 to 335 KIAS for four minutes.

What could be done if auto deployment of the ADG did not occur with the failure of all AC power in flight?

Pulling the ADG manual-deploy handle at the bottom of the center pedestal would manually deploy the ADG. Deployment will be indicated by an ADG shown on the ELEC synoptic page, and EMER PWR ONLY EICAS message.

What will the ADG power when it deploys with all other AC power inoperative in flight?

The ADG bus powers the AC ESS BUS and the ACMP 3B hydraulic pump. The AC ESS BUS then powers the ESS TRU 1, DC ESS BUS, and the BATT BUS.

When will automatic deployment of the ADG in flight occur?

When all three generators are not providing AC power and AC BUS 1 and 2 are not powered.

When the ADG is released manually or automatically, what is releasing the ADG from its uplock?

The wet and dry models have different methods. With the dry model, the ADG control unit sends an electrical signal to the release solenoid. With the wet model, the ADG control unit sends an electrical signal to fire a squib that is part of the ADG up-lock mechanism.

Explain the PWR TXFR OVERRIDE switch?

After ADG deployment it may be possible to get an aircraft generator on line. The generator would then be powering most of the AC buses and the PWR TXFR OVERRIDE switch would transfer the AC ESS BUS to the aircraft generator. It would also de-activate the hydraulic pump ACMP 3B.

Explain the LAMP/UNIT switch on the ADG AUTO DEPLOY CONTROL panel.

- LAMP position: This checks the light bulb on the AUTO DEPLOY CONTROL unit.

- UNIT position: AC BUS 1 and 2 must be powered and two generators must be operating for an accurate test. In the TEST position the control unit will check the logic circuit of the control unit and the transfer relay.

What are the sources of DC electrical power?

- 5 transformer rectifier units (TRUs)

- Two NiCad batteries

- DC external power

Where is the DC external power receptacle located?

The DC external power receptacle is near the right engine on the aft fuselage.

How many DC buses are in the electrical system and name them?

10 total:

1. DC BUS 1 (main)

2. DC BUS 2 (main)

3. DC ESS (essential) BUS

4. DC SERV (service) BUS

5. DC UTIL (utility) BUS

6. DC UTIL (utility) BUS

7. DC BATT BUS (battery)

8. DC EMER BUS (emergency)

9. MAIN BATT DIRECT BUS

10. APU BATT DIRECT BUS

How do the TRUs provide DC power?

The TRUs provide 28 volt DC by transforming and rectifying the supplied 115-volt AC electrical power.

What is the amp rating of the TRUs?

100 amps

What are the five TRUs?

1. TRU 1

2. TRU 2

3. ESS (essential) TRU 1

4. ESS (essential) TRU 2

5. SERV (service) TRU

What buses does TRU 1 supply power to?

It normally supplies BUS 1 and UTIL BUS 1.

TRU 2 supplies power to what buses?

It normally supplies BUS 2 and UTIL BUS 2.

ESS TRU 1 supplies power to what buses?

It normally supplies the ESS BUS and BATT BUS.

ESS TRU 2 supplies power to what buses?

It normally supplies the ESS BUS and BATT BUS.

The SERV TRU normally supplies power to what buses?

It normally supplies the SERV BUS.

What CB panels are DC BUS 1 and DC BUS 2 located on?

DC bus 1 is located on the CB panel one behind the captain's seat and DC bus 2 is located on the CB panel two behind the first officer's seat.

What equipment does the DC ESS BUS supply power to?

The DC ESS BUS supplies the equipment essential for flight.

What buses normally power the DC ESS BUS?

ESS TRU 1 and 2 normally power the DC ESS BUS.

Explain how the DC ESS BUS is protected so it will always be powered?

If the ESS TRU 2 fails, the SERV TRU will be used to power the ESS DC BUS. If ESS TRU 1, 2 and SERV TRU fail, the DC ESS BUS can be powered from the APU BATT DIR BUS and the MAIN BATT DIR BUS.

When the ADG is deployed during a complete AC power failure, the AC ESS BUS powers ESS TRU 1, which in turn powers the DC ESS BUS.

What does the DC SERV BUS supply power to?

The external navigation lights including the beacon and lighting in the passenger cabin.

What powers the DC SERV BUS?

Normally by the SERV TRU.

What bus powers the reading lights at the passenger service units?

DC utility buses 1 and 2. DC utility bus 1 powers the left side of the cabin and DC utility bus 2 powers the right side of the cabin.

Which TRUs power the DC UTIL Buses?

TRU 1 powers DC UTIL BUS 1 and TRU 2 powers DC UTIL BUS 2.

What powers the DC UTIL BUS 1 or 2 when the associated TRU that normally powers the bus fails?

When the TRU that is associated with the DC UTIL BUS fails, that DC UTIL BUS will be load shed to reduce DC electrical loading. The DC tie contractors accomplish the load shedding.

What is the purpose of the DC TIE contactors?

There are two purposes that the tie contactors provide at the same time. First, when there is a TRU failure, the DC tie associated with that TRU is closed to provide the affected bus with other power. Second, at the same time the DC tie will interrupt power to other buses to prevent overloading of the TRUs.

What happens to the DC TIE if there is a failure of TRU 1?

The SERV TRU would provide power with TIE 1 closing and UTIL BUS 1 being shed to prevent overloading of the TRUs. If the SERV TRU were not available, both DC tie 1 and 2 would close allowing TRU 2 to power BUS 1.

This allows two sources of backup power to DC BUS 1 and 2, the SERV BUS and TRU 1 to backup DC BUS 2 and TRU 2 to backup DC BUS 1.

What is the purpose of the TIE 1 and TIE 2 switch lights on the electrical power services panel?

These switch lights allow the pilot to select the associated DC tie contactors closed. When pressed, the switch light illuminating white and a status message on the EICAS indicates closing of the TIE.

Explain the ESS TIE switch light on the electrical panel.

When selected, the switch light will illuminate white and a DC ESS TIE CLSD status message will appear on the EICAS. The ESS TIE will close connecting the SERV TRU to the ESS BUS.

Can the SERV TRU supply power to DC BUS 1 or 2 when the ESS TIE switch light is selected?

No

What condition will cause the ESS TIE to automatically close?

There is no automatic function of the essential tie contactor.

What is the purpose of the DC power supply from the batteries?

The batteries supply emergency DC power if there is a failure of all AC power and the ADG did not deploy in flight. They also supply power to start the APU and get the APU generator on line.

Explain the primary batteries of the aircraft.

The batteries are located in the aft equipment bay and are two nickel-cadmium (nicad) batteries. The APU battery is a 24 volt 43 ampere/hour and the main battery is 24 volt 17 ampere/hour.

What maintains a constant state of charge on the batteries?

Located in the aft equipment bay there are two individual battery chargers. They will charge the batteries as long as the UTIL BUS 1 and 2 are on line.

What are the four buses that the batteries supply DC electrical power to?

1. DC BATT BUS

2. DC EMER BUS

3. APU BATT DIR BUS

4. MAIN BATT DIR BUS

What buses do the batteries directly power?

The main battery directly powers the MAIN BATT DIR BUS and the APU battery powers the APU BATT DIR BUS.

What CB panel are the MAIN BATT DIR BUS and the APU BATT DIR BUS located?

Both are on CB panel 5.

Explain the DC Emergency Bus.

This bus is connected to the APU DIR BATT BUS and the BATT BUS, which means it is continuously powered. This bus provides power to the engine and APU fire extinguishers and power to the fuel and hydraulic shut off valves (SOV).

Why is the DC emergency bus not depicted on the DC electrical page?

It will be displayed only when the bus is not powered because of a fault.

What are the power sources for the BATT BUS?

With AC power available, ESS TRU 1 and 2 power it. If the ESS TRU 1 and 2 were not available, the SERV TRU could power the BATT BUS if the ESS TIE was selected closed by the pilots. When the BATTERY MASTER switch is selected to ON, the BATTERY BUS is directly connected to both the APU and MAIN Battery Direct buses. The Battery Bus is critical to flight.

In flight with the ADG deployed and operating, what buses is it powering?

The ADG is powering the AC ESS BUS which then powers ESS TRU 1 and that in turn powers the DC ESS BUS and the BATT BUS.

While in flight with all generators failed and the ADG deployed but not generating power, what buses will be powered?

The main and APU batteries will power the DC BATT BUS and the DC ESS BUS.

While in flight with the Main and APU batteries the only source of power, how long will they provide power?

Approximately 30 minutes.

Why does the checklist require the ADG Manual Deploy Handle to remain pulled out?

If it is pushed back in, with the weight on wheels signal at touchdown the emergency tie contactors will receive this signal and the battery power will be removed from the DC ESS BUS.

At about 80 knots the ADG will not be providing power and the only power left is the battery which will power the DC ESS Bus only if the ADG handle is pulled.

How will you know if external DC power is available?

If the parameters are correct, the green AVAIL light will illuminate in the DC switch light on the flight deck electrical power services panel.

What happens when you press the external DC power switch light when the green AVAIL light is illuminated?

The external DC power will provide power to the MAIN BATT DIR BUS and the APU BAT DIR BUS. This will cause the white IN USE portion of the switch light to illuminate. The batteries will now not be connected to the battery direct buses.

What is required to connect the BATT BUS to external DC power?

The battery master selected ON.

What does the amber FAIL portion of the AUTO XFER switch light indicate?

Bus priority is to ensure that AC BUS 1 and 2 are powered. This light indicates that a transfer has failed. It really is an AUTO XFER inhibit switch light and indicates it did its job because the situation called for the transfer not to occur.

What does the OFF portion of the AUTO XFER switch light indicate?

The switch light has been selected and the bus priority is inhibited.

What does the FAULT light in the IDG switch light indicate?

The FAULT light indicates there is an oil problem, low oil pressure or high oil temp. The IDG will end up disconnecting automatically or you will have to select the IDG disconnect.

What does the DC service switch on the flight deck electrical panel do?

The DC Service switch powers the DC SERV bus for servicing the aircraft. It will power the NAV and Beacon lights for towing the aircraft.

What bus is the STAB trim channel 2 on?

The STAB trim channel 2 is on the DC ESS bus. This is why it is selected when the ADG is deployed.

Why is the left engine started first when only external DC power is available?

- The left fuel pump is DC powered.

- The oil gauge works on the left engine when only DC power is available.

What buses will the external AC switch light on the external services panel power?

This switch light will power the UTIL and SERV buses.

What do you lose when you press DC Tie 1 or 2?

The associated UTIL bus will be load shed.

Why is the EMER bus not shown on the ELEC synoptic page?

The EMER Bus is displayed on the ELEC page only when there is a problem with it.

When is the EMERG bus powered?

The EMERG Bus is always powered because it is a hot bus.

When would you have to close all three DC ties?

Never close all three DC ties at the same time. If you do, everything left of the SERV TRU will be lost. Only the DC ESS BUS and the BATT BUS will be powered.

The situation where you could get in trouble is when TRU 1 and 2 are lost so DC TIE 1 and 2 automatically close. The SERV TRU is now powering DC bus 1 and 2. If you select the ESS TIE closed because ESS TRU 2 failed, all you are doing is providing a backup to the ESS Bus.

The DC TIE switches require power on both sides of the TIE to open and close and power on both sides was just lost. This is an important point to remember and is why the ESS TIE is not automatic.

After ADG deployment, an engine generator is brought on line. You press the power transfer override switch to return the ESS bus and hydraulic 3B to normal AC power but nothing happens. What could cause this?

The ADG manual-deploy handle needs to be stowed for this to work.

chapter 6

Engine

What type of engines does the CRJ have?

General Electric CF34-3A1 or CF34-3B1.

What is the normal takeoff thrust rating?

8,729 pounds per engine.

How much thrust is produced when the APR is activated?

9,220 pounds, which is a 2% increase.

Explain the general makeup of the N1 and N2 sections of the engine.

The N1 section is a single stage fan connected to a 4-stage low-pressure turbine by a shaft. The N2 section is a 14-stage axial flow compressor connected to a 2 stage high-pressure turbine by a shaft.

What section of the engine drives the accessory gearbox?

The N2 compressor.

What decreases the engines ability to create thrust?

- Increase in pressure altitude.

- Increase in temperature.

How are the N1 and N2 sections connected?

The N1 and N2 sections are independent.

Explain the two paths that air can take through the engine.

- Bypass air: This air is accelerated by the N1 fan and sent around the engine nacelle.

- Core air: This air is accelerated by the N1 fan and then sent to the N2 section where it is compressed, fuel is added and then ignited. This burned, accelerated gas then drives the N2 and N1 turbine.

The bypass N1 airflow on takeoff produces how much of the thrust?

80%

Do the thrust reversers direct the core or bypass airflow forward to assist in braking?

The bypass airflow is diverted forward.

What improves the efficiency of the N2 compressor and protects against stall and surge damage?

A Variable Geometry Compressor (VG). The VG changes the angle of attack of the inlet guide vanes and the first five stages of the stator vanes. The changing of the angle of attack optimizes the airflow for best efficiency. The Fuel Control Unit (FCU) uses fuel to hydraulically change the angle of the vanes.

Where is the ITT measured?

Between the high and low-pressure turbine.

What equipment does the accessory gearbox drive?

- Alternator, which powers the N1 control amplifier.

- Lubrication pumps for the engine.

- Hydraulic pump.

- Fuel control unit and engine fuel pump.

- Integral drive generator (IDG).

What are the different jobs of the fuel system?

- Provide motive flow to the main ejector pumps and scavenge pumps.

- Lubricate and actuate servos in the FCU.

- Cool engine oil.

- Adjust the variable geometry compressor linkage.

What are the different ways to stop fuel flow to the engine?

- Shut off the thrust lever.

- Press the fire switch light on the glare shield panel.

What is the purpose of the fuel oil heat exchanger?

The exchanger warms the fuel and cools the engine oil.

Are any of the fuel filters displayed on the fuel synoptic page?

Yes, one for each engine.

How would you know the fuel temperature at the fuel filter?

The temperature is displayed next to the fuel filter on the fuel synoptic page.

What occurs when a fuel filter is clogged?

The fuel will bypass the filter. There will be an EICAS caution message along with an amber fuel filter on the fuel synoptic page.

What controls the VG Inlet Guide Vanes and Stator Vanes of the engine compressor?

The Fuel control unit (FCU).

Explain N2 speed control.

During low power settings up to 79% N1, the FCU hydro-mechanically controls the N2 speed of the engine. This is so that matched movement of the thrust levers produces fairly matched N2 rpm.

Explain N1 speed control.

Above 79% N1 the N1 control amplifier controls engine rpm. The engine speed switches have to be on for this to occur. This is so that matched movement of the thrust levers produces fairly matched N1 rpm.

What would happen at cruise flight if the ENG SPEED switches were turned off?

There would be an increase in RPM and ITT that could exceed limitations.

How would you know if there were an impending oil filter bypass?

There are no EICAS indications. In the aft equipment bay there are associated indications.

How would you know if a chip detector had detected some metal in the engine oil?

There are no EICAS indications. In the aft equipment bay there are associated indications.

How can the engine oil be checked and replenished?

Located on the captain's side panel is the ENGINE OIL LEVEL control panel. The level can be tested and filled from this panel.

Explain the engine oil test.

Press the START/STOP switch light for the oil test. If an engine is low, the REFILL, light will illuminate. The white STOP light will illuminate after the test if both engine oil levels are normal.

What does the amber FAIL light in the engine oil level LH or RH switch light indicate?

This will illuminate during and engine oil level check to indicate a failure of an oil level sensor.

What type of engine starter does the CRJ have?

An air turbine starter.

What two things are required to open the starter valve and engage the starter?

- DC power

- 10th stage bleed air

What does the air turbine starter actually drive?

It drives a gearbox that drives the N2 section.

What are the sources that can provide 10th stage bleed air to start the engines?

- External air cart.

- APU.

- The opposite engine bleed air, which is called a cross bleed start.

At what N2 speed does the start valve close automatically?

55% N2

What is the purpose of the start valve?

The valve meters the amount of air to the starter, which controls the rate of engine acceleration.

If just the engine starter was activated and no fuel added, what maximum N2% would the starter achieve?

30%

Does the N2 need to be zero before engaging the starter again after a start attempt?

No, the starter can be engaged up to 55% N2 rpm.

What are the two ways the start valve will close?

- Press the STOP switch light on the start ignition panel.

- When the N2 RPM is above 55%.

What valves open when the engine START switch light is pressed?

- L and R 10th stage bleed SOVs.

- 10th stage ISOL valve.

- Start valve for the engine that is being started.

What are the starter limitations?

Start #	Time Engaged	Cool Down Time
1	60 sec	10 sec
2	60 sec	10 sec
3 & after	60 sec	5 min

What are the dry motoring starter limitations?

Start #	Time Engaged	Cool Down Time
1	90 sec	5 min
2	30 sec	5 min

What does pressing IGNITION A or B do?

Activates the ignition A or B on both engines. The green ARM light in the switch light will illuminate.

What happens when the CONT ignition switch light is pressed?

The A and B ignition system on both engines is activated.

Are the ignition systems DC or AC powered?

Ignition A and B are AC ignition systems. Ignition system B has a static inverter that turns DC in to AC power.

What are the power sources for ignition A and B?

- The AC Essential Bus powers ignition A.

- The Battery Bus powers ignition B through a static inverter. This is why ignition B is used when only DC power is available for start.

During engine start, when is the ignition energized?

It is energized when the starter is engaged and is turned off when at starter cutout.

Does continuous ignition activate ignition A or B?

Both are energized.

When must continuous ignition be used?

- Takeoff with a 10-knot or greater crosswind component.

- Takeoff and landings on contaminated runways.

- Flight in moderate or heavier rain.

- Flight in the vicinity of thunderstorms.

- Flight in moderate or heavier turbulence.

What determines automatic activation of the continuous ignition?

This is based on angle-of-attack (AOA) as sensed by the stall-warning computer through the AOA vane.

If a thrust reverser deploys in flight, what system helps to minimize asymmetrical thrust?

The affected thrust lever will be mechanically retarded to idle.

What systems monitor thrust lever position to determine its operation?

- Ground lift dump system

- Cabin pressurization

- Landing gear warning system

- Takeoff configuration system

What does pressing the TOGA switch do while on the ground in addition to controlling the FD bars?

Updates the FMS position.

When are the thrust reversers most effective?

At high ground speeds.

What conditions must be met for the thrust reversers to operate?

- Weight-on-wheels.

- 14th stage bleed air valve opened.

- Thrust reverser switches in the armed position.

What is needed to operate the power drive unit (PDU) that moves the translating cowls?

14th stage bleed air, which means the 14th stage bleed air valves must be selected open.

Can the thrust levers be moved forward after the thrust reverser levers have been activated?

No, the thrust levers are now locked at idle.

Is engine core or bypass thrust used to provide reverse thrust?

Bypass fan air is redirected forward to provide reverse thrust.

Can the thrust reversers be activated in flight?

No, they are locked out.

Explain the thrust reverser emergency stow?

If the thrust reverser unlocks in flight the pilot should press the affected emergency stow switch light on the panel. This will direct 14th stage bleed air to the PDU and stow the reverser.

What happens upon touch down or a rejected takeoff if the 14th stage bleed is being used for anti-icing and the thrust reversers are activated?

The thrust reversers are activated and the anti-ice systems are deactivated. The anti-ice system will begin to operate when the thrust reversers are stowed.

Can flex thrust be used with cowl and/or wing anti-ice systems on?

No

Can the pilot select a thrust setting on the thrust limit page of the FMS other than what the actual configuration is? (Example: The 10th stage bleed open is selected and the pilot selects cowl anti-ice on the thrust limit page).

Another setting can be selected to see the thrust limit. The value on the FMS page will be amber.

On a single FMS installation what does the message on the CDU, FMS-EFD N1 DISAGREE indicate?

This has to do with the Wrap-Around Comparator. The EICAS displays the N1 value and this value is also sent to the FMS. When the FMS receives this value it compares it to its own generated value. If the values are different by more than 0.04%, the FMS will display an FMS-EFD N1 DISAGREE message on the CDU and the primary page N1 is removed.

On a single FMS installation, explain the message on the CDU ADC TEMP DISAGREE.

This indicates that the two ADC's have a temperature difference of more than 3 degrees as measured by the FMS temperature comparator. The N1 indication on the EICAS primary page is removed.

On a dual FMS installation, explain the FMS CDU message FMS-FMS N1 DISAGREE.

Dual FMS installations are equipped with a N1 Cross FMC Comparator. Each FMS figures its own N1 value and if these values are different by more than 0.03%, the FMS-FMS N1 DISAGREE message will appear. The N1 reference will be removed.

On a dual FMS installation, explain the FMS CDU message F DISAGREE.

This indicates the EICAS Comparator has detected a N1 difference of 0.9% between the two FMS units because the N1 Cross Comparator failed to sense the difference at 0.03%. When the N1 Cross FMS comparator fails to detect a difference in the N1 values the EICAS Comparator will at 0.9%. The N1 indication on the EICAS primary will be removed.

How long is the automatic performance reserve system (APR) armed after takeoff?

The APR is armed for 5 min. after takeoff. The APR arms when N1 rpm is above 79%.

When will the APR activate?

When an engine N1 decreases to 67.6% and the APR is armed, the APR will activate. The APR sends the signal to both engines to increase N1 by 2%.

Is the APR available if the ENG SPEED switches are selected OFF?

No, the APR is controlled by the N1 speed control.

How much does the APR increase thrust?

The APR system increases thrust approximately 2% N1, which is about 500 pounds of thrust for each engine.

When an engine fails and the APR activates, does the APR system only send a signal to the engine still operating?

It sends the signal to increase N1 to both engines, but since the failed engine is below 79% N1 it is in N2 speed control by the FCU.

How is the arming of the APR system indicated?

There is a green APR ARM displayed on the EICAS as the thrust levers are advanced to takeoff.

Can the APR system be activated on a go-around?

No, it is only armed and activated on takeoff with an engine failure.

When the APR is activated due to an engine failure, what EICAS messages are associated with the APR?

The green APR ARMED EICAS message is removed, and a green APR appears in the N1 gauge.

When should the APR system be tested?

The test must be done on the ground with both engines running.

What indications is the pilot looking for during the APR test?

The pilot should look for the green APR icon in both N1 gauges and a green APR TEST OK on the EICAS. Note: there are two positions to this test switch.

During takeoff an engine failure occurs while using a reduced thrust of 85% N1. Will the APR system advance the N1 to full takeoff thrust plus 2% N1?

The APR will advance the N1 2% to 87%. There is nothing wrong with the pilot advancing the thrust lever to full takeoff thrust plus 2% N1. Performance was calculated at 85% and the runway data indicated that an engine failure at V1 at reduced thrust would meet the performance requirements.

Which engine components are monitored for vibration?

The N2 core section and the N1 fan section.

When will the N1 fan vibration gauges be displayed on the EICAS?

The gauges will be displayed when oil pressures are normal and both engines are running.

How will the pilots be alerted to an excessive N1 vibration?

The N1 vibration gauges will change from green to amber but there is no EICAS message. There will probably be a noticeable sound and maybe a vibration felt.

What is the trigger point for the N1 vibration gauges to turn amber?

2.7 mils

When will the N1 vibration gauges be removed from the EICAS?

When the oil pressure is low or if either engine is shut down.

How are the N2 vibration levels displayed?

The N2 vibration level is not presented like the N1 VIB gauges. The N2 vibration is always monitored but only displayed when it is outside a target limit.

When there is excessive N2 vibration, how will it be displayed?

There is no EICAS caution message, but there will be an amber VIB in the N2 gauge. The N2 gauge will also turn amber.

How is the vibration monitoring system tested?

A VIB test switch on the ENGINE CONTROL panel performs the test. This will display the VIB gauges and indicate an excessive vibration condition.

With the N1 ENG SPEED switches are selected OFF, what will not be working?

APR and N1 speed control will not work.

When should the engine oil check be accomplished?

The check should be done 15 minutes to 2 hours after engine shutdown.

What are the indications of a hot start?

There is a rapid rise in ITT and a red HOT icon will be displayed inside the ITT gauge. The ITT pointer will also turn red.

What are the indications of a hung start?

N2 stagnation at about 40% with a fairly rapid rise in ITT.

What are the color ranges of the oil pressure displays?

Red: 0-25 PSI
Green: 26-115 PSI
Amber: 116-156 PSI

When will the fuel flow displays turn amber?

They are only presented in green.

What are the color ranges of the oil temperature indications?

Green: -40-154 deg. C
Amber: 155 to 162 deg. C
Red: 163 deg. C and above

At what oil pressure indication will the N1 vibration gauges be removed?

25 PSI

Is AC power required to start the engine?

No, DC power and air from the 10th stage manifold is required to open the start valve.

What are the two external air sources used for starting the engines?

- Bottle

- Huffer

DC power is the only power available (APU deferred) to start the engines. What are some things you should be thinking about?

- Use ignition B since it converts DC power to AC power through an inverter.

- Start the left engine first because it will have an oil pressure indication.

- After starting the #1 engine establish AC engine generator power and start the right with the external air.

- If passengers still need to be boarded after starting the #2 engine and generator #2 is online, shut down #1 and board the passengers.

- Possible no starter cutout at 55% N2.

What is the correct procedure for aborting a hot start?

1. Thrust lever shutoff.

2. Ignition off.

3. Dry motor until the ITT is below 120 C or starter limit of 60 seconds, which ever occurs first.

chapter 7

Environmental Control

What stage of the engine do the packs get air from?

The 10th stage is where pack air is extracted.

Where are the air condition units located?

They are located in the aft equipment bay.

Where is the air distributed that comes from the left and right pack?

The left pack will normally supply the cockpit and the right pack will supply the cabin.

What regulates the pressure of the air from the 10th stage before it enters the pack?

Due to the extreme pressure of the air from the 10th stage, the air could damage the pack if the pressure was not reduced. This is the job of the pack pressure regulating shutoff valve (PRSOV) and is used to reduce the pressure of the air before it enters the pack.

What would occur if the PRSOV failed?

The valve would close, the pack would shut down and a pack high pressure EICAS message would be displayed.

How does the PRSOV help a single pack supply sufficient pressure to the flight deck and the cabin during single pack operations?

There are two pressure settings, one for dual pack and one for single pack. When two packs are available, the PRSOVs reduce the 10th stage pressure to a normal pressure. During single pack operations the single PRSOV will increase the operating pressure, which will permit the single pack to supply the cabin and flight deck with sufficient airflow. It will not be at the same volume as with both packs operating.

What is the single pack operating altitude limit?

25,000 feet

What cools the hot air for the air conditioning system?

An air cycle machine and heat exchangers cools the hot compressed air.

What is the purpose of the ram air scoop at the base of the vertical stabilizer?

Air enters this scoop and is used as the cooling means for the air-to-air heat exchangers. The ram air flows across the pre-cooler and dual heat exchangers thus cooling the pack air. The cooling ram air exits through the vents located on the lower right and left sides of the fuselage in the aft area. When the aircraft is on the ground there is no ram air to enter the scoop, so a fan that is driven by the air cycle machine draws the air in the scoop.

Explain the RAM AIR switch light on the air conditioning panel.

This switch light controls the ram air shut off valve. When selected open, it will direct air that enters the ram air scoop to enter the left distribution duct. This duct will ventilate the flight deck and cool the EFIS and EICAS equipment. Only a small portion will ventilate the cabin. This switch will only work with the packs off.

What are the sources of air conditioning bleed air?

- APU

- Engines

- External air cart

What is the altitude limit for extracting bleed air from the APU for air conditioning? What will happen if the APU is used for bleed air above his altitude?

The limit is 15,000 feet. If this altitude is exceeded the EICAS caution message APU BLEED AIR ON will appear.

Where is the left pack air distributed?

The air will be sent to the flight deck gaspers, vents and side console outlets. It will also be used for EICAS and EFIS display cooling.

Where is the right pack air distributed?

It is distributed to the floor outlets in the passenger cabin, lavatory, galley, and the gaspers on the PSUs.

Where is the cabin air exhausted?

The air sent under the floor to outflow valves on the aft pressure bulkhead.

Where is the low-pressure ground air connection?

It is located behind the wing on the right side of the aircraft.

Does the low-pressure air cart supply air to the packs for the aircraft cooling?

No, the air is sent directly to the distribution manifold, which then travels to all the outlets.

What must be done before the low-pressure air can be turned on?

The main cabin door or avionics bay door must be open.

Explain how suitable airflow is maintained in the cargo bay.

A fan draws re-circulated passenger cabin exhaust air from under the floor into the cargo bay to maintain suitable airflow and temperature.

In addition to the re-circulated air, there is an optional automatic temperature control that uses right fresh pack air for cooling and an electric heater for increasing temperature. This controller maintains the temperature in the cargo bay that is better suited for live animals.

What happens to the cargo SOVs if the cargo smoke detectors detect smoke?

The SOVs used for circulation of air will automatically close. If COND AIR is selected, the SOV from right pack for air-conditioned air will close and the heater turned off.

What happens when FAN is selected on the cargo fan switch?

A fan is energized and the cargo re-circulation and exhaust shutoff valves are opened. Air is then taken from the passenger cabin exhaust duct and used to supply suitable airflow to the cargo bay.

What happens when COND AIR is selected on the cargo fan switch?

An SOV is opened that allows right pack air into the cargo fan ducting. The air then flows to a heater before flowing to the cargo bay. Temperature is controlled by a heater cycling on and off as commanded by a thermostat located in the exhaust ducting.

Is overheat protection provided in the cargo bay?

Overheat protection is provided only with the condition air option selected.

What does an amber CARGO OVHT on the EICAS indicate?

This EICAS message will only occur if the conditioned air option is installed. If the cargo bay temperature reaches 35 degrees C and conditioned air is selected, an overheat condition is detected. The heater is de-energized and the EICAS CARGO OVHT is presented. The CARGO COND AIR switch should be selected to FAN.

When there is a CARGO OVHT with the condition air option, and the cargo fan switch is selected from COND AIR to FAN, what does this do?

This takes the power away from the over temperature circuitry and removes the indication from the EICAS display. This cargo intake and exhaust SOV's are still open so there is suitable airflow. It matches the condition since the heater is automatically turned off.

How is cabin pressurization maintained?

By the two outflow valves controlling the rate the air leaves the vessel.

What happens to the cargo air when one or both of the cargo smoke detectors detect smoke?

The cargo intake and exhaust SOVs close, the cargo fan shuts down, the optional condition air valve closes and the heater shuts down.

Briefly explain how the outflow valves operate.

There are two outflow valves located on the aft bulkhead that control the amount of air leaving the aircraft. Vacuum pressure from a jet pump driven from the 10th stage bleed air manifold is used to open the outflow valves, which are held closed by springs.

Explain the automatic mode of the cabin pressure controllers (CPCs).

In the automatic mode the outflow safety valves open via CPCs sending electrical signals to control the vacuum. The CPC will open and close the outflow valves to control cabin pressure.

Explain the manual mode of the cabin pressurization.

The vacuum to the outflow safety valves is controlled manually by controls on the CABIN PRESS control panel. The checklist will guide you in how to control the cabin pressure.

What differential pressure range is maintained during aircraft operations?

The outflow valves will open and close to maintain a differential pressure from 0 to 8.4 PSID.

Explain the protection against excessive differential pressure.

If the pressure differential reaches 8.6 +/- 1, an aural warning "cabin pressure" will sound and both outflow valves will automatically open to bring the differential pressure back to the normal range. If there is a negative pressure differential that reaches -0.5 PSID, the outflow valves will automatically open to bring the pressure into the normal range. There is no EICAS indication for exceeding the negative pressure differential of -0.5.

In the AUTO mode of the cabin pressurization, what controls the pressurization?

There are two CPCs, which while in AUTO only one CPC will control all phases of pressurization at a given time. The CPC that is not active will be in standby and will become active if there is a failure of the active CPC.

What indicates which CPC is active?

It is identified on the ECS page.

When will the active CPC become the standby CPC?

The active CPC can be changed any time manually by pressing the PRESS CONTROL switch light on the CABIN PRESS control panel two times. The active will also become the standby three minutes after landing. The standby will return to the active upon the next landing.

What are the automatic modes of the CPCs?

- Ground mode

- Pre-pressurization mode

- Takeoff abort mode

- Climb mode

- Flight abort mode

- Cruise mode

- Descent mode

- Landing mode

Explain the ground mode of the CPC.

After AC power is applied the CPC completes a self-test. The ground mode will start at the completion of the self-test and the safety valves will be driven full open to provide ventilation on the ground. 10th stage bleed air is need for the valves to driven open.

Explain the pre-pressurization mode of the CPC.

This mode is activated when the thrust levers are set for takeoff. The outflow valves start to close and the cabin will be pressurized to approximately 150 feet below field elevation. The pre-pressurization of the aircraft eliminates any noticeable pressure bumps.

Explain the takeoff abort mode of the CPC.

When the thrust levers are retarded during a rejected takeoff the CPC will bring the cabin back to field elevation at 500 fpm for 20 seconds and then drive the outflow valves full open. The CPC will then be in the ground mode.

Explain the climb mode of the CPC.

The CPC controls cabin pressurization based on the selected landing field elevation and a theoretical schedule of cabin altitude versus aircraft altitude. The profile that the cabin climbs on is based on the aircraft's rate of climb, which that profile is about 300-500 fpm.

Explain the flight abort mode.

This mode is armed within the first 10 minutes of the flight and the aircraft is still below 6000 feet. The purpose of this mode is so the pilot does not have to reset the landing elevation when returning to the departure field. The mode is activated with a decent of 1000 fpm or more.

Explain the cruise mode of the CPC.

There is an assigned cabin altitude for every cruising altitude. Once in cruise mode the descent mode is armed automatically.

Explain the descent mode of the CPC.

The cabin will descend based on the rate of descent and flight time remaining. Flight time remaining is based on information received from the ADCs. The cabin will normally descend at 300 fpm until the cabin altitude is 150 below the selected landing field elevation.

Explain the landing mode of the CPC.

When the PSEU senses weight on wheels and the thrust levers are at idle the CPC will transfer from the descent mode to landing mode. In the landing mode CPC will climb the cabin at 500 fpm for 60 seconds and then enter the ground mode. Three minutes after landing the active CPC will become the standby.

Are any electrical controls involved in manual pressurization?

None

Explain how you would manually control the pressurization.

Pressing the PRESS CONT switch light once on the CABIN PRESS control panel will illuminate the green MAN light in the switch light and activate manual pressurization control. Using the MAN RATE knob and the MAN ALT selector valve, the pilot can manually control the vacuum pressure to the outflow safety valves and therefore control cabin pressurization. Selecting up or down on the MAN ALT selector will climb or descend the cabin at the rate selected on the MAN RATE knob. The EICAS Primary, ECS and Status page will provide pressurization information.

Begin manual pressurization control with rate knob at full decrease to avoid large pressure changes at manual activation.

What does the red FAULT in the PRESS CONT switch light indicate?

The light indicates that both CPCs have failed.

Explain what happens when the EMER DEPRESS switch light is pressed on the CABIN PRESS control panel.

The active CPC will drive both outflow safety valves fully open. If the aircraft is below 14,250 feet the aircraft will completely depressurize and if it is above 14,250 feet the aircraft cabin will climb and maintain 14,250 +/-750 feet. Both CPCs have emergency depressurization circuitry that is not part of the normal system so it will not be affected by normal system failures.

What is the purpose of the Cabin Pressure Acquisition Module (CPAM)?

The CPAM provides pressurization data for display on the EICAS after communicating with the data concentrator units (DCU). The EICAS indications include differential pressure (Δ), cabin altitude (CALT) and cabin rate of climb or descent (RATE).

When the cabin altitude exceeds 8,500 feet the CPAM will display an amber CABIN ALT on the EICAS. When the cabin altitude exceeds 10,000 feet the CPAM will display a red CABIN ALT on the EICAS and an aural "cabin pressure" alert.

When cabin altitude exceeds 10,000 feet the CPAM will illuminate the NO SMOKING/ FASTEN SEAT BELT sign if those switches are in AUTO.

When the cabin altitude reaches 14,000 feet the CPAM will send the signal to drop the passenger oxygen masks.

Will any of the normal CPAM functions occur if the CPAM fails?

The CPC that is in standby will generate all the EICAS messages if the CPAM fails, but the illumination of the SEATBELT/ NO SMOKING signs and dropping of the passenger masks will not occur.

Note: This would automatically occur if the CPAM were operating when the cabin altitude exceeds 10,000 and 14,000 feet respectively. For the SEATBELT/ NO SMOKING signs to illuminate automatically, the switches would need to be in AUTO.

How are the EFIS and EICAS cathode ray tubes (CRTs) cooled?

The CRTs are cooled by air-conditioned pack air distributed by fans.

Explain the DISPLAY FAN selector on the Display and ARINC control panel.

The CRTs for the EFIS and EICAS require 3 AC powered fans to ensure there is proper airflow for display cooling. If a CRT overheats it has internal overheat protection which will shut down the affected CRT. The three fans are controlled by the PSEU and weight-on-wheels.

One fan is used in flight and the other fan is used on the ground. The switching is accomplished by the PSEU and the weight on wheel function. If #1 fails in flight, the #2 fan can be selected by the FLT ALTN position of the DSPLY FAN knob. If both fans fail, the STBY fan can be selected. This will activate the standby fan that draws air from the floor area near the rudder pedals and is unfiltered air. The GND ALTN position will activate the other fan if the main ground fan fails.

Failure is indicated by an amber DISPLAY COOL on the EICAS.

Explain the operation of the ARINC FAN switch.

Cooling air is needed across the aeronautical radio incorporated (ARINC) radios on the lower avionics equipment rack. There are two fans used for this, one for flight and one on the ground. Switching is a function of the PSEU WOW signal sent for takeoff and landing.

The air used for cooling is taken from under the cabin floor and is the recalculated passenger cabin air.

If fan #1 for in flight fails, #2 can be selected by moving the ARINC FAN switch to FLT ALTN. If the aircraft is on the ground and fan #2 fails, fan #1 can be select by selecting GRD ALTN. Failure is indicated by an amber ARINC COOL on the EICAS.

Explain the avionics exhaust fan.

There is a single fan that operates when the AC buses are powered. It extracts the exhaust air from the CRTs, the ARINC racks, the pedestal panel and the avionics bay.

When the passenger door or the service door is open the exhaust air is discharged through the overboard exhaust valve. If this valve fails open when the doors are closed, an amber OVBD COOL will be displayed on the EICAS.

With the passenger and service doors closed, the overboard exhaust valve closes. The inboard exhaust valve opens to send the air into the fuselage. A white EICAS INBD COOL FAIL will indicate failure of this valve.

Will there be any warning if there is a low airflow for avionics cooling?

There will be an EICAS caution message of DISPLAY COOL if there is a duct blockage or fan failure by the low flow detectors.

What does the amber FAIL light in the left or right pack switch light indicate?

Pack has shut down due to overpressure or over temperature.

At what pack temperature does the amber EICAS message L PACK HI TEMP appear?

When pack temperature reaches 85 degrees C.

What supplies the cooling air for the heat exchangers?

The ram air scoop at the base of the vertical stabilizer is where cooling air enters.

When would you use ram air ventilation?

When both packs have failed in flight ram air ventilation would be used.

Where is the flight compartment exhaust air routed?

Under the floor through the avionics bay to outflow valves on the aft pressure bulkhead.

How is cabin air outflow controlled?

Cabin air outflow is controlled by two outflow safety valves.

What is the source of the vacuum for the outflow valves?

A jet pump and 10th stage bleed air.

What happens when you press the pressurization control switch once?

Manual mode is selected.

What happens when the manual cabin altitude regulator is selected up with the manual pressurization is selected?

The outflow valves will open and the cabin altitude will climb.

When manual pressurization is selected where will the pressurization readouts be displayed?

The primary page of the EICAS and the ECS page will display pressurization information.

When will the cabin altitude aural warning be heard?

When cabin altitude is above 10,000 feet.

What happens if the CPAM fails?

The standby CPC takes over but the CPC can't drop the masks or illuminate the NO SMOKING/SEATBELT SIGNS.

The CPAM would normally illuminate the SMOKING/SEATBELT SIGNS if the cabin altitude exceeds 10,000 feet. And the CPAM would also send the signal to drop the passenger masks at 14,000 feet.

chapter 8

Fire & Overheat Protection

What are the four areas with fire and overheat detection?

- Engine

- Jet pipe and pylons

- APU

- Main landing gear

What two areas have smoke detection systems?

- Cargo bay

- Lavatory

What areas of the engine have fire and overheat protection?

Fire and/or overheat protection are provided in the jet pipe, nacelle, and pylon areas. These are divided into two zones, the engine area (ENG), which is the core of the engine and second is the jet area (JET), which is the jet pipe and pylon.

Is fire extinguishing provided in both the ENG and JET zones of the engine?

Fire extinguishing is provided in the ENG zone. Only detection is provided in the JET zone.

What ducting is contained in the JET zone?

10th stage and 14th stage bleed air ducting are contained in this zone.

What in the engine actually detects the fire or overheat condition?

There are two detection loops labeled A and B, which are connected to a control unit. As there is an increase in temperature i.e. fire, the electrical resistance of the insulator decreases with an increase in temperature to a trip point at which there will be a fire or overheat indication generated.

How are the detection loops arranged in the engine zone?

The detection loops are located in the aft engine core and the side of the cowl panel that is near the fuselage.

How are the loops arranged in the jet zone?

The loops are around the jet pipe and it runs along the 10th and 14th stage bleed air ducting in the pylon areas.

What are the two benefits of the dual loop detection systems?

- Minimize false fire warnings. This is because both loops must sense the fire or overheat condition before a fire is detected.

- The aircraft can be dispatched with a loop that is inoperative and still provide fire and overheat protection.

Explain the operation of the fire detection control unit.

This unit monitors the electrical resistance of the loops. Both loops must sense the same decrease in electrical resistance at the same time for the fire detection control unit to send the signal to the EICAS.

This unit also monitors the loops for malfunctions and if a malfunction is detected in a loop, the second loop maintains the capability of detecting an overheat condition or fire. The failed loop will no longer be used.

What do the fire extinguisher bottles contain?

The bottles contain Halon and are pressurized with nitrogen.

Where are the engine fire extinguishers located?

The extinguishers are located in the aft equipment bay below the APU enclosure.

Will the left engine fire bottle only discharge into the left engine?

No, both bottles can be discharged into one engine. This is determined by which fire switch is pressed.

What is the purpose of the FIRE DETECTION control panel?

To select a single loop if one has failed so the aircraft can still be dispatched. The panel can also be used to test the Fire and Overheat Detection System.

Explain the three positions of the ENG, JET and APU selector switches on the FIRE DETECTION control panel.

- A: The system only uses loop A for fire and overheat detection.

- B: The system uses only loop B for fire and overheat detection.

- BOTH: The fire and overheat detection system will compare the loops for fire and overheat conditions.

What happens when the LH or RH FIRE PUSH switch light are pressed?

- Fuel feed SOV is closed.

- Bleed air SOV is closed.

- Hydraulic SOV is closed.

- Engine driven generator is taken off line.

- Both fire extinguisher bottle squibs are armed, both BOTTLE ARMED PUSH TO DISCH switch lights illuminate.

What happens when a BOTTLE ARMED PUSH TO DISCH switch light is pressed after being activated by the FIRE switch light?

An electrical current fires the squib on the selected bottle. The Halon is directed into the engine nacelle on the side of the selected fire switch.

What determines which engine nacelle the fire extinguisher bottle will be discharged into?

The engine nacelle is determined by which FIRE PUSH switch light is pressed.

How many loops are used to detect a fire or overheat condition of the APU?

Two loops of the same design as the engine loops.

What monitors the fire loops of the APU?

The fire detection control unit monitors the fire loops of the APU.

Explain the two modes of operation of the APU fire detection?

- *Ground*: When there is a fire condition with the aircraft on the ground, the APU will shut down automatically. Five seconds after shut down, the APU fire bottle discharges into the APU enclosure automatically and a horn will sound.

- *Flight*: When there is a fire detected, the APU will shut down automatically. The Halon will not discharge automatically.

How many squibs does the APU fire bottle have?

Two

Where are the APU fire detection loops located?

The loops are around the inside of the APU enclosure.

Where is the fire extinguisher bottle for the APU located?

It is located in the aft equipment bay, beside the APU enclosure.

What happens when the APU FIRE PUSH switch light is pressed?

- APU fuel feed SOV is closed.

- APU is shutdown by closing the fuel solenoid valve.

- APU LCV is closed.

- APU generator is taken off line.

- Both squibs are armed and the BOTTLE ARMED PUSH TO DISCH switch light is illuminated.

What happens when the APU BOTTLE ARMED PUSH TO DISCH switch light is pressed after it is activated?

When pressed, an electrical current fires the two squibs and pressurized Halon is released into the APU enclosure.

Where is the APU fire warning horn located?

The horn is located in the aft equipment bay under the APU battery.

What is used for fire protection in the cargo bay?

Two fire bottles in the aft equipment bay and two smoke detectors in the cargo bay protect the cargo bay.

Explain the cargo smoke detectors?

Two smoke detectors are installed in the ceiling of the cargo compartment. As the name states, they monitor the compartment for the presence of smoke. If one or both detect smoke, it will illuminate the CARGO SMOKE on the EICAS and all airflow will stop to the cargo bay.

How is airflow automatically stopped to the cargo bay if one or both smoke detectors detect smoke?

The following stops airflow:

- Cargo exhaust SOV is closed.

- The optional heater shuts down if installed.

- The air conditioning SOV is closed if installed.

- Cargo compartment fan stops.

- Re-circulation SOV is closed.

Are the smoke detectors susceptible to false alarms?

Mobile radios or cell phones on the ground near the detectors or exhaust from equipment can set them off.

What is the extinguishing agent in the cargo fire extinguisher bottles?

Halon

How many squibs does each cargo-extinguishing bottle have?

2 each

What is the difference between the cargo fire extinguisher bottles?

They discharge the Halon at different rates. The squibs are fired at the same time but bottle one discharges the Halon immediately and bottle two discharges the Halon slowly. The purpose of bottle two discharging slowly is to maintain a presence of Halon for an extended amount of time.

What is the purpose of the CARGO FIREX control panel?

The switches on this panel arm the cargo bay fire extinguishing system and will discharge the fire extinguishing bottles.

What will happen if the CARGO SMOKE PUSH switches are pushed on the CARGO FIREX panel?

The switch lights illuminate when the smoke detector(s) detect smoke. When pressed the squibs for the extinguisher bottles will be armed and both BOTTLE ARMED PUSH TO DISCH switch lights illuminate. The cargo fan stops, re-circulation SOV closes, the optional heater shuts down, optional air conditioning SOV closes, and the exhaust SOV closes. This all seals the cargo bay.

What happens when the BOTTLE ARMED PUSH TO DISCH switch light on the CARGO FIREX panel is pressed after being armed?

Pressing just one switch light will fire all four squibs discharging both bottles into the cargo bay. Normally you will press both switch lights.

What does the CARGO BOTTLE test switch on the FIRE DETECTION panel do?

The switch is used to test the fire extinguishing and smoke detection systems for the cargo bay.

Where is the smoke detector located in the lavatory?

The smoke detector is located on the ceiling.

What happens when the lavatory smoke detector is tested by pressing the self-test switch on the detector?

- The detector will sound an alarm.

- A red light on the detector will illuminate.

- The EICAS will display an amber SMOKE TOILET.

When the lavatory smoke detector detects smoke, what happens?

SMOKE TOILET will be displayed on the primary page of the EICAS and an alarm on the detector will sound.

Can the lavatory smoke detector be reset?

Yes, press the test/reset button on the smoke detector.

Is there any fire extinguishing in the lavatory?

Fire extinguishing is only provided in the waste bin.

Explain the fire extinguisher in the waste bin.

There are two heat sensitive plugs that melt and release the Halon into the bin. The bottle is located on a bracket beside the waste bin.

Where is the fire extinguisher located on the flight deck?

The fire extinguisher is located behind the co-pilot's seat. It is a Halon fire extinguisher.

What detects an overheat condition in the main landing gear bay?

A single detection loop in the top of each wheel bin that is monitored by the overheat detection unit.

How does the loop in the landing gear bay detect an overheat condition?

The loop has an outer metal cover with two internal wires separated by insulating material. As heat is increased the resistance of the insulator decreases. At a certain point a signal will be sent to the monitor and a overheat indication will be displayed.

How is a main landing gear bay overheat brought to the pilots attention?

A MLG BAY OVHT warning message will be displayed on the EICAS and an aural alert will sound, "gear bay overheat".

What will happen if the gear bay overheat detection loop fails?

The control unit continuously monitors the loop and if the loop is not working properly, an amber EICAS message MLG OVHT FAIL is presented.

Explain the MLG BAY OVHT switch on the landing gear control panel.

When held in the OVHT position, a simulated overheat condition in the main landing gear bay will be indicated by a red MLG BAY OVHT warning message with an aural alert.

Explain the OVHT TEST WARN FAIL switch on the landing gear control panel.

This switch will simulate the failure of the main landing gear bay overheat detection system. This test will generate an amber MLG OVHT FAIL caution message.

Explain the TEST WARN / FAIL switch on the FIRE DETECTION panel.

The WARN position tests all loops for an open or short circuit. When the WARN position is selected look for the following messages:

- APU FIRE

- LE JETPIPE OVHT

- R JETPIPE OVHT

- R ENG FIRE

- L ENG FIRE

If you continue to hold the switch in the WARN position, the following five amber messages will appear:

- HYD SOV 1 OPEN

- HYD SOV 2 OPEN

- L ENG SOV OPEN

- R ENG SOV OPEN

- APU SOV OPEN (this will appear if the APU is operating)

In the FAIL position the control unit is tested for its ability to discriminate between a real fire and a false fire indication. Look for the following five amber messages:

- L JET OVHT FAIL

- R JET OVHT FAIL

- L FIRE FAIL

- R FIRE FAIL

- APU FIRE FAIL

Explain the ENGINE BOTTLE switch position 1 and 2 on the FIREX MONITOR panel.

This switch is used to check the serviceability of the squibs on engine bottles 1 and 2.

Explain the APU BOTTLE test switch on the FIREX MONITOR panel.

The test position tests the serviceability of the squibs on the APU bottle. Hold the switch in the test position and look for a green SQUIB 1 and SQUIB 2 on the EICAS. Release the switch and the messages should disappear then come back and then disappear again.

The second time the green messages come back it is testing the automatic function of the squibs.

What is the purpose of the CARGO BOTTLE test switch on the FIREX MONITOR panel?

The purpose is to test the fire extinguishing and smoke detection system of the cargo compartment.

- TEST 1: Look for a red EICAS warning CARGO SMOKE, advisory CARGO SQUIB 1 and aural "SMOKE". Both CARGO SMOKE PUSH switch lights and the normal BOTTLE ARMED PUSH TO DISCH switch light on the CARGO FIREX panel will be illuminated.

- TEST 2: This test is the same as 1 except on the CARGO FIREX panel; the standby BOTTLE ARMED PUSH TO DISCH switch light is illuminated.

Where is fire detection and extinguishing provided?

Left and right engine nacelles, APU, and cargo areas. The lavatory has smoke detection with extinguishing in the waste bin.

What will happen if there is an APU fire on the ground?

The APU will shut down, automatically discharge the extinguisher bottle, sound the horn and display an EICAS message.

How is the lavatory trash bin extinguisher discharged?

The heat sensitive plugs melts on the extinguisher to discharge the Halon into the trash bin.

How can the fire bell on the flight deck be silenced?

By pressing the master warning switch light.

What indications will you receive if loop A is in normal condition and loop B is detecting a fire?

The indication will be an amber L or R FIRE FAIL EICAS message.

What would happen if one engine fire loop were detecting a short or power failure and the other loop is detecting a fire?

An engine fire warning would occur. When the system sees that one loop is bad, it will just monitor the good loop.

Which areas only have overheat detection?

The main wheel wells, jet pipe and pylon areas.

How long does it take to completely discharge both cargo fire extinguish bottles?

It takes a total of 45 minutes to discharge both bottles. One bottle discharges over 45 minutes to maintain a level of Halon in the cargo compartment.

What would be the warning if there were a bleed air leak in the pylon?

The warning would be a JET PIPE OVHT on the associated side.

If one loop senses a fire and the other doesn't, what is the EICAS message?

The message will be L or R FIRE FAIL.

If a fire detection loop were cut would it still detect a fire?

Yes it would detect a fire condition. The cut wire would be caught during the fire detection test.

chapter 9

Flight Controls

What is the purpose of the spoilerons?

The spoilerons aid the ailerons to provide greater roll response at low airspeeds.

How are the aileron, elevator and rudder surfaces moved?

Through the controls on the flight deck, control movement is transmitted via cable and/or push rods to the power control units (PCU) that will hydraulically move the surface.

How many PCUs are on each aileron?

2

Explain how the aileron control system is actually two separate systems.

The pilot controls the left aileron and the co-pilot controls the right aileron. Under normal operations the aileron controls are interconnected with coordinated movement of the control surfaces.

How are the spoilerons moved?

Hydraulically, but electronically controlled by fly-by-wire.

Explain the Spoiler Electronic Control Units (SECU 1 and SECU 2).

The SECUs receive an electrical signal from the control wheels when they are moved. The SECUs then take this control movement information with other information like airspeed to determine the amount of spoileron deflection. The spoilerons will operate only on the wing that goes down to assist with roll.

What keeps the aileron control surface from fluttering in flight if all hydraulic pressure is lost to a PCU?

Each aileron has a flutter damper to prevent flutter.

What serves as a gust lock for the ailerons on the ground?

The flutter damper along with the PCUs. Hydraulic pressure is locked in the system to prevent movement.

What is the purpose of the aileron disconnect function (roll disconnect)?

Allows the crew to separate the left control wheel and associated cable system from the right. This can be useful in case of a jammed aileron control system or a PCU runaway.

What happens when the ROLL DISC handle is pulled?

The control wheel interconnect (torque tube) is separated and it will advise the SECU that the interconnect torque tube has been disconnected. The pilot has control of the left aileron and the right spoileron. The co-pilot has control of the right aileron and left spoileron.

Twenty seconds after pulling the ROLL DISC handle, the SECU will illuminate the two amber ROLL SEL lights on the glare shield to illuminate and display the EICAS caution SPOILERONS ROLL message. The pilots then need to determine which side is not jammed and select the ROLL SEL switch light on the non-jammed side and this will provide the flying pilot with the use of the onside spoileron.

Selecting the ROLL SEL will remove the amber ROLL SEL lights on the glare shield and the EICAS caution. The green PLT ROLL CMD or CPLT ROLL CMD will appear on glare shield and on the EICAS depending which ROL SEL switch light was selected.

What happens if an aileron PCU causes an un-commanded roll, with a runaway aileron?

A bungee breakout switch with the aileron system that is running away sends a signal to the SECU. The SECU then will command both spoilerons to respond to control wheel inputs and will present on the EICAS PLT ROLL CMD or CPLT ROLL CMD. The SECU will also illuminate the green ROLL SEL switch light on the glare shield in front of the pilot that should take control prior to ordering the ROLL DISC handle to be pulled.

What are the two situations that would require the use of the ROLL DISC handle?

- A jammed aileron.

- An un-commanded displacement of an aileron PCU.

How many PCUs power the rudder?

3

How is rudder jam protection provided?

Anti-jam/breakout protection (spring tension breakout) is provided to both sets of pedals. In case of a jammed rudder control, both sets of pedals will remain working but additional pedal force will be required to move the rudder.

Is there any gust lock protection for the rudder?

When the hydraulic systems are depressurized, the trapped fluid will prevent rudder movement.

How many degrees will the rudder move?

The rudder will move 25 degrees in both directions.

What is the purpose of the yaw dampers (YD)?

They improve directional stability and turn coordination. If these oscillations were not corrected by the YDs it could cause dutch roll.

Are the yaw dampers connected to the autopilot?

The yaw dampers operate separately.

What commands the movement of the yaw dampers?

The flight control computers (FCC) operate the yaw dampers. FCC 1 controls yaw damper 1 and FCC 2 control yaw damper 2.

What is the function of the YD 1 and YD 2 button on the YAW DAMPER panel?

They engage the associated yaw damper.

How are the yaw dampers disengaged?

- The yaw damper DISC button on the YAW DAMPER panel.

- If the YD channel fails.

- Upon landing.

What occurs if both YDs fail?

If the autopilot is engaged it will disconnect and their will be an EICAS caution message that both YDs are off line.

How is pitch control provided?

By the elevators and assisted by a moveable horizontal stabilizer.

How many PCUs are provided for each elevator?

There are three PCUs for each elevator.

How are the left and right elevators connected?

During normal operations the left and right elevators are connected but can be separated in case of one being jammed. The two systems are separate except for the connection. The pilot controls the left elevator and the co-pilot controls the right.

Explain the flutter dampers on the elevators.

Each elevator has two flutter dampers that prevent flutter in flight if there is a complete loss of hydraulic pressure at a PCU. They also serve as a gust lock while on the ground.

What happens when the PITCH DISC handle is pulled and turned?

The interconnection between the two elevators is removed. The operable control surface will be controlled by the pilot or co-pilot controls. If both surfaces are operable, the captain will control the left elevator and the FO will control the right elevator.

When the PITCH DISC handle is pulled and turned will there be any EICAS message?

No

What happens if there is a jammed elevator PCU?

It will be overpowered by the other two PCUs on that elevator.

Explain how aileron trim is accomplished?

Both switches of the AIL TRIM must be pushed left or right to actuate the aileron trim. When the switch is actuated, signals are sent to reposition the aileron cables; this will cause the control wheels to move.

Do all of the aileron PCUs need to be working for the aileron trim to work properly?

Minimum of 1 out of 3 PCUs needs to be operative.

What is the color of the neutral position of the aileron and rudder trim on the EICAS STATUS and F/CTL page?

With the aircraft on the ground the neutral indication will be green. In the air the indication will be white regardless of trim position.

What happens when the RUD TRIM switch is turned left or right?

This switch moves the rudder control cables to move the rudder surface. NL and NR stands for nose left and nose right.

Will actuating the rudder trim cause the rudder peddles to move?

Due to the position of the rudder trim actuator, the trim will not cause the pedals to move.

Do all three rudder PCUs need to be operative for the rudder trim to move the rudder surface?

Only one PCU needs to be operative to actuate the rudder trim.

What provides horizontal pitch trim?

The trim switches on the control yoke vary the horizontals stabilizers angle of incidence. It moves from +2 degrees to -13 degrees (nose up).

How does the horizontal stabilizer mechanically move?

Two electric motors drive a screw jack, which moves the horizontal stabilizer.

What happens when STAB TRIM CH 1 and CH 2 switches are pressed?

Pressing these switches engages channel 1 and 2 of the Horizontal Stabilizer Trim Control Unit (HSTCU). They are engage only switches.

What happens if a HSTCU motor has a runaway?

To prevent this each trim motor has a brake. If there is a runaway, the brake will engage to stop the runaway.

Where does the HSTCU receive inputs?

- Autopilot (AFCS)

- Mach Trim System

- Control wheel trim switches

How is the STAB TRIM disengaged?

The only way the pilots can disconnect the stabilizer trim is by the pitch/trim disconnect button on either control wheel. The horizontal stabilizer is monitored and if there is a fault, the stab trim will be disengaged automatically. This will be indicated on the EICAS by a white status message STAB CH 1 OR 2 INOP if one channel fails and an amber caution message STAB TRIM if both channels fail.

What is the normal takeoff range of the stab trim on the EICAS?

Normal takeoff is 3 to 9 units and this will produce a green trim indication.

What is the stabilizer trim priority order?

1. Pilot manual trim

2. Co-pilot manual trim

3. Autopilot

4. Auto trim

5. Mach trim

What is auto trim?

When the flaps are moving between 0-20 degrees up or down with no other inputs from the autopilot or the pilots, there is a change in the aerodynamic center of pressure because of the flap movement. The auto trim will compensate for these changes by trimming the horizontal stabilizer.

Explain the different rates at which the flaps move.

- Pilot manual trim moves the stabilizer at the highest rate of movement.

- Copilot manual trim moves the stabilizer at the highest rate of movement.

- Autopilot has two rates of stabilizer movement. A high rate occurs when the flaps are extending or retracting and a low rate when the flaps are not moving.

- Mach trim moves the stabilizer at the slowest rate.

What is happening if you hear a clacker sound?

This could be a possible runaway trim. If the stabilizer trim is in motion for more than 3 seconds the clacker will sound. This can also occur if a pilot activates the stabilizer trim for more than 3 seconds.

What is the purpose of the Mach trim?

As Mach speed increases the Mach trim will make allowances for the rearward shift of the aerodynamic center of pressure. A negative stick force gradient and a decrease in longitudinal stability (Mach tuck) would occur above Mach 0.4 while hand flying if this correction did not occur.

What sends the signal for the need for Mach trim?

Both FCCs must demand trim before the HSTCU will adjust the stabilizer as a function of Mach number with the autopilot not engaged and hand flying the airplane.

What must be operating for the Mach trim to function?

Both channels of the HSTCU must be powered and at least one stab trim channel engaged.

How do you engage the Mach trim?

Press the MACH TRIM switch light. Both channels of the HSTCU must be powered and at least one stab trim channel engaged.

How would you disengage the Mach trim?

Pressing the MACH TRIM switch light after it has been engaged or press the stab trim disconnect on either control wheel.

What is the design of the flaps?

The flaps are double - slotted fowler flaps that move rearward and down.

Explain the bent up trailing edge (BUTE) doors on the outboard flaps?

The BUTE doors direct airflow over the leading edge vanes when the flaps are extending. Fixed leading edge vanes and cams operate the BUTE doors.

When the inboard flaps are extended, how is air directed over the flaps?

Spring-loaded leading edge vanes automatically extend when the flaps are deployed.

Explain what happens when the flap lever is moved from 0-8 degrees.

An electrical command is sent from the flap electronic control unit (FECU) to start flap movement. The flap brakes are released and the two AC power drive units (PDU) turn the flap gearbox, which rotates flex shafts to move the flap ball screw actuators. When 8 degrees is reached the PDUs are de-energized and the flap brakes are applied. This is the same process for any flap movement.

When will the flap position indicator appear on the EICAS primary page?

When at least one of the following occur:

- The flaps are greater than zero degrees.

- Brake temperature monitoring system (BTMS) is in the red range.

- The landing gear is not up and locked.

When will the flap indication be removed from the EICAS primary page?

When all of the following occur in flight:

- Gear is up and locked.

- BTMS is normal, not in red.

- The flaps are up.

What EICAS page will <u>always</u> display flap position?

EICAS F/CTL page.

When will the flaps operate at half speed?

If there is a failure of a single PDU or one FECU channel. It will be indicated as a FLAP HALFSPEED status message.

What will happen if the FECU detects a fault?

An amber EICAS FLAPS FAIL message will appear and the flaps will stop.

What are the types of spoiler panels located on the top of each wing?

The panels are the spoileron, flight spoiler, and outboard and inboard ground spoiler for a total of four on each wing.

What is the job of the flight spoilers?

They provide speed control and lift dumping.

What is the degree range of the flight spoilers?

Any position between 0 to 50 degrees.

What happens if the flight spoilers are deployed in flight and the thrust levers are advanced?

When deployed there is a green EICAS message FLT SPLRS. As the thrust levers are advanced above 70% N1 the green EICAS message is replaced with amber FLT SPLRS caution message.

What spoilers make up the Ground Lift Dump System (GLD)?

The flight spoilers, spoilerons, the inboard and outboard ground spoilers make up the GLD system. All spoiler panels make up the GLD system.

What controls the extension/retraction of the spoilerons, flight spoilers and GLD system?

SECU 1 and 2.

What is the purpose of the GLD system?

The system aids during touchdown and after a rejected takeoff to spoil lift and increase drag to help stop the aircraft.

Where do the SECUs get information to operate the automatic and manual modes of the GLD system?

- The engine N1 signals.

- Proximity Sensor Electronic Unit (PSEU), weight on wheels function.

- Thrust lever position micro switches.

- Wheel speed from the anti-skid control unit.

- The radio altimeter.

What conditions are necessary for the GLD to be armed for takeoff when the spoilers switch is in the AUTO position?

- Left or right engine greater than 79% N1.

- Wheel speed greater than 45 knots.

What happens to the GLD system if a touch and go landing is necessary?

If the thrust levers are advanced the GLD will retract and the system will re-arm.

What conditions are necessary on landing for the GLD system to deploy the *ground and flight spoilers* automatically?

Spoilers switch in MAN ARM or AUTO. L and R thrust levers at idle or L or R N1 less than 40% *and* two of the following three:

- L *or* R MLG WOW.

- Wheel speed greater than 16 KTS.

- Radio altimeter less than 5 feet.

What conditions are necessary for the GLD system to deploy the *spoilerons* automatically?

- The SPOILERS switch in MAN ARM or AUTO.

- L *and* R thrust levers at idle or L and R N1 less than 40%.

- L *and* R MLG WOW.

One of the following two:

- Wheel speed greater than 16 knots.

- Radio altimeter less than 5 feet.

How are the GLD panels automatically retracted after landing?

The following conditions must be met:

- Left or right engine less than minimum takeoff setting.

- Inboard and outboard wheel speed less than 45 knots for at least 10 seconds.

- Aircraft must be on the ground for at least 40 seconds.

How is the GLD manually retracted after landing?

Selecting the SPOILERS switch to MAN DISARM.

What does the takeoff configuration warning system monitor?

The position of the following:

- Flaps

- Flight spoilers

- Autopilot

- Parking brake

- Aileron trim

- Rudder trim

- Horizontal stabilizer trims

When is the takeoff configuration warning system armed?

When the aircraft is on the ground.

What indicates the aircraft is in takeoff configuration?

The green T/O CONFIG O/K advisory message on the EICAS status page indicates the aircraft is configured for takeoff. This message is removed at aircraft rotation or anytime T/O configuration is not met.

What happens if the takeoff configuration warning system senses an unsafe takeoff configuration?

When *both* engines are above 70% N1, the master warning will flash, aural alerts sound and warning messages are presented on the EICAS. Depends on what caused the alert.

How can a takeoff configuration warning be canceled?

Cancellation only occurs by retarding the thrust levers or correcting the configuration problem that created the warning.

What monitors the aircraft systems for correct configuration and operation?

The proximity sensing system (PSS). The PSS consists of the proximity sensing electronic unit (PSEU), which receives information from the proximity switches, proximity sensors and micro switches. The PSEU then sends the information to command the operation of other aircraft subsystems.

What is the purpose of the stall protection system (SPS)?

If there is an impending stall this system provides aural, visual, and tactile warnings. It will also try to prevent the stall with a stick pusher.

What does the SPS monitor?

- Left and right angle of attack (AOA) vanes

- Lateral acceleration through the AHRS system

- Flap position

- Weight on wheels

- Mach speed - Mach transducers and ASCs 1 and 2

How is Mach data provided to the SPS?

Mach data is supplied to the SPS computer via the Mach transducers. This data is used for Mach compensation of the aircraft's stall margin. The ADCs provide secondary Mach data to the SPS computer.

What is the purpose of the pressure selector valves for the Mach transducers on the pilot and co-pilot's side panel?

Each switch is connected to two pressure selector valves and is used to isolate the Mach transducers from the pitot/static system.

What does the SPS do when a high angle of attack (AOA) is approached?

First the continuous (CONT) ignition is activated and if the AOA continues to increase, the stick shaker is activated followed by the autopilot disengaging. If after all of this the AOA is still increased, the stick pusher is activated, the STALL switch lights on the glare shield flash and the warbler sounds.

What happens to the SPS system if the AOA is increased rapidly?

If the AOA is increased at a rate greater than 1 degree per second, the SPS will lower the point of stall warning activation. The SPS will give the stall warnings at a lower AOA.

Once the stick pusher is activated, what will disconnect it?

- If less than 0.5G is sensed by an acceleration switch.

- Press and hold either the pilot or co-pilot autopilot/stick pusher disconnect switch (AP/SP DISC).

- Select either STALL PTCT PUSHER switch to OFF.

Does the AP/SP DISC button need to just be pressed and released to disengage the stick pusher?

It must be pressed and held to disengage the stick pusher as long as the activation is enabled. Otherwise if the AP/SP DISC button is release and the pusher conditions are met the SPS system will reengage the stick pusher.

If only one STALL PTCT PUSHER switch is selected ON, will the stick pusher engage if the activation point was met?

Both of the STALL PTCT PUSHER switches must be selected ON.

How is the SPS system tested?

The test is accomplished on the ground by pressing either STALL switch light on the glare shield. Any fault will be sent to the DCU for aural and/or visual annunciation.

What helps the crew in directional control with a jammed rudder?

The anti-jam system of the rudder, the spring tension breakout. It will take a little more rudder pressure from the pilot, but the pilot will be able to override the jammed rudder.

What hydraulic systems power the flight controls?

- *System 1*: Rudder, elevator, left aileron, left spoileron, flight spoilers and outboard ground spoiler.

- *System 2*: Rudder, elevator, right aileron, right spoileron, flight spoilers, inboard ground spoiler.

- *System 3*: Rudder, elevator, both ailerons, both spoilerons.

What is the purpose of the aileron bungee breakout switch?

When there is an uncommanded displacement of an aileron PCU, the switch with the runaway aileron will send a signal to the SECU. The SECU will command both spoilerons to respond to the single control wheel.

The green PLT/CPLT ROLL light on the glare shield will illuminate in front of the pilot that as control.

When will the glare shield amber ROLL SELECT switch lights illuminate?

It will illuminate 20 seconds after the roll disconnect handle has been pulled. The pilot and copilot's cable runs are now separated. After the ROLL SEL switch on the side with the non-jammed aileron is selected, the amber ROLL SEL is removed.

What EICAS message will appear if one channel of the FECU fails?

The message will be Flap Half Speed.

How is a jammed elevator corrected?

The jammed elevator PCU will be overridden by the other two PCUs.

What problem is the PITCH DISC handle used to correct?

This is used for cable problems.

What is done to correct a rudder cable jam?

The pilot just needs to apply increased rudder peddle force. The other two PCUs will override the jammed PCU.

Flight Instruments

What formats can be selected on the multi-function display (MFD)?

- Radar

- FMS plan map

- TCAS

- FMS map

- Navaid sector

- HSI

What is the purpose of the Display Reversionary Panel (DRP)?

The switch is used to change the format on the associated MFD to a PFD or EICAS format.

What is the purpose of the Source Selector Panel?

If there is a failure of an air data computer, attitude/heading computer, EICAS or display control panel (DCP), this panel will allow an alternate source for the system to be selected.

Explain the ATT HDG switch on the source selector panel.

- *Norm*: The pilot and co-pilot electronic flight displays receive data from onside AHRS.

- *Position 1 and 2*: The pilot's and copilot's electronic flight displays receive data from AHRS 1 in position 1 and AHRS 2 in position 2. There will be an amber message on the PFD and or MFD displaying the source.

Explain the AIR DATA switch on the source selector panel.

- *Norm*: The pilot and co-pilot electronic flight displays receive data from the on-side air data computer (ADC).

- *Position 1 and 2*: The pilot and copilot's electronic flight displays will display data from ADC 1 in position 1 and ADC 2 in position 2. On both PFDs there will be displayed an amber ADC 1 or 2 depending on selection.

Explain the DSPL CONT switch on the source selector panel.

- *Norm:* The pilot and copilot's electronic flight displays are controlled by the respective DCPs.

- *Position 1 and 2:* In position 1, the pilot and copilot's electronic flight displays are controlled by the pilot's DCP. In position 2, the copilot's DCP controls the pilot and copilot's electronic flight displays. On both MFDs and PFDs there will be an amber source message.

Explain the EICAS switch on the source selector panel.

When either ED1 or ED2 EICAS display fails, the remaining operative ED can display all EICAS pages.

Example: ED1 fails and the primary page automatically transfers to ED2 and this makes the ECP inactive. To regain the use of the ECP, select ED2 on the source selector panel. This will reactivate the ECP and all pages can now be displayed on ED2. If ED2 fails, selecting ED1 allows all pages to be viewed on ED1 through the ECP.

What is the name of the panel that allows airspeeds to be set?

The Air Data Reference Panel (ARP).

What is the name of the panel that allows the NAV SOURCE to be set?

The Display Control Panel (DCP).

What is the name of the panel that allows autopilot commands to be set?

The Flight Control Panel (FCP).

Explain the EFIS Comparison Monitor.

The primary flight display (PFD) continuously monitors itself in comparison to the other PFD. When the EFIS PFDs detect a comparison disagreement between each other an amber EFIS COMP MON is displayed on the primary page of the EICAS. The data message associated with the disagreement will flash for 5 seconds on the PFDs and then stay steady as long as the comparison error exists.

What does an amber HDG message on the PFDs indicate?

There is a difference of more than 6 degrees between each AHRS.

What does an amber ROL message on the PFDs indicate?

There is a difference of more than 4 degrees roll or 3 degrees if the glide slope is captured.

What does the amber PIT message on the PFDs indicate?

There is a difference of more than 4 degrees pitch or 3 degrees after the glide slope is captured.

What does the amber IAS message on the PFDs indicate?

There is a difference of more than 10 knots between PFDs.

What does the amber ALT message on the PFDs indicate?

There is more than 60 feet difference between PFDs.

What does the amber LOC message on the PFDs indicate?

There is a difference between the localizer receivers.

What does the amber GS message on the PFDs indicate?

There is a difference between the glide slope receivers.

What does the amber RA message on the PFDs indicate?

There is a difference between the radio altimeters below 1000 feet AGL.

What systems do the pitot static system supply information to?

- Air data computers (ADC)

- Stall protection system (SPS)

- Cabin pressure acquisition module (CPAM)

- Standby air data system (ADS)

- Mach transducer of the stall protection system

Where is the total air temperature (TAT) probe located?

Located under the copilot's side window.

Explain the TAT probe.

Total air temperature is determined by this probe and supplied to the ADCs. The ADCs then use the TAT information to calculate and display on the EFIS the true airspeed (TAS), static air temperature (SAT), and total air temperature (TAT).

How is the DH/MDA removed from the PFD?

When displayed, it can be removed by pressing the center of the DH/MDA knob.

How can individual speeds be removed from the PFD?

When the speed is selected, pressing the center of the SPEED REFS knob will remove the speed displayed at that time.

What would indicate a good test of the radio altimeter?

Press the RA TEST button and the RA should indicate 50 feet. When the button is release, the reading should return to 0.

How is the speed reference manually changed between Mach and IAS?

Press the center of the SPEED KNOB.

Explain the low and high-speed cues.

The checkerboard at the top and bottom of the airspeed scale indicates these cues. The top indicates Vmo/Mmo and the bottom indicates a calculated airspeed of 1.06Vs.

What is the green line that moves around on the airspeed scale?

This is the Low Speed Awareness Cue, which indicates 1.26Vs.

Explain the airspeed Trend Vector.

The trend vector moves in response to the aircraft acceleration or deceleration. It indicates the predicted speed in 10 seconds.

When will the Mach window appear in the top left corner of the PFD?

When aircraft speed is above Mach .45 the Mach window will appear. It will be removed when the Mach is below .40 Mach.

What is the range of the of the barometric altitude readout?

-1,000 to 50,000 feet

What happens to the altitude alert when the aircraft is passing through 1,000 feet above or below the pre-selected altitude?

There is an aural tone and the pre selected altitude bugs flash.

What happens when the aircraft deviates from the selected altitude?

When the deviation reaches 200 feet from the pre-selected altitude, an aural tone is heard and the pre selected altitude indicators flash yellow. When it is only a minor deviation the pre-selected altitude flashes magenta.

What is meant when the pre-selected altitude turns cyan?

The latitude tracking between the ADCs is outside tolerances.

What is the range of the MDA setting?

0 to 15,000 feet

What is the range of the vertical speed field?

The scale range is 0 to +/- 4,000 fpm. The digital readout ranges from 0 to 15,000 feet.

What else can be displayed on the VSI other than vertical speed?

TCAS advisory deviations.

What is the range of the radio altitude display?

-20 to 2,500 feet AGL

What are the different colors of the radio altitude display?

The digital readout is green from decision height (DH) to 2,500 feet and amber equal or lower than DH.

What happens if the radio altitude fails?

An RA in a red box appears and the RA tape and digit readouts are removed.

Where is altitude information presented other than the normal radio digital radio readout provided?

Next to the altitude tape is a scale, which indicates altitudes from 0 to 1,100 feet. The indication is green but turns amber at DH and then turns green again at touchdown.

What is the digital range selection of the decision height display?

0 to 999

What will happen if the ADC airspeed, vertical speed or altitude fails?

Red air data flags will replace the system information on the PFD.

What warning is provided if the aircraft descends to a negative altitude?

A yellow NEG will be displayed next to the altimeter on the PFD.

What system supplies the attitude and heading information?

The attitude and heading reference system (AHRS).

What components does the AHRS system consist of?

The AHRS system is made up of 2 computers, 2 flux detector units and 2 remote compensator units.

What panel provides AHRS mode selections?

The COMPASS control panel.

When would you use the DG mode on the COMPASS control panel?

When the aircraft is in an area of magnetic field disruptions or failure of heading information from the AHRS system. It is not intended for long-term use.

How long does it take for initialization of the AHRS system?

Initialization occurs automatically when electrical power is established with the aircraft stationary. In MAG mode initialization takes approximately 70 seconds and 10 minutes in DG mode.

What provides rate and acceleration data for the AHRS computer?

There are two sensors for each AHRS computer. These sensors have four pairs of piezoelectric accelerometer sensors that are on a rotating wheel.

Explain the SLEW switch on the COMPASS control panel.

The switch is operational in DG and MAG mode. In MAG mode it will cause the displayed heading to move but it will move back to its original position when the slew switch is released. In DG mode the SLEW switch will cause the heading to slew in the direction selected and it will stay when released.

What happens when DG is selected on the COMPASS control panel?

The flux detector data no longer provides heading information.

Can the aircraft be moved during AHRS ground alignment process?

The aircraft should not be moved. The PFD will display the message ATT/HDG ALIGNING DO NOT TAXI during the alignment process. If there is motion detected during the alignment process, the AHRS will re-initialize.

Can the AHRS conduct the alignment process in flight?

Airborne alignment is possible and will take 10 to 35 seconds. This would be needed if there were a power interruption. Most of the same flags on the PFD that appear during the ground alignment will appear in flight. The aircraft should remain in straight and level flight.

What is the color of the glide slope triangle when showing onside and cross-side data?

The triangle is green for on side and amber for cross side.

What is the value of the two dots above and below the reference line for vertical deviation?

Each dot is 1/4 degree.

When the vertical deviation on the glide slope display senses excessive vertical deviation the triangle flashes in amber color. How can this flashing amber be corrected?

The flashing amber diamond can only be canceled when the condition is corrected.

What happens if the glide slope information is not valid?

There will be a red-boxed GS flag in the position of the glide slope pointer and scale.

What is the purpose of the amber alpha margin indicator (AMI) during a wind shear indication?

The AMI represents the maximum pitch attitude allowed up to 30 degrees. This pitch attitude is just before the activation of the stick shaker.

How long is the AMI displayed during a wind shear warning?

It is displayed a minimum of 60 seconds or until the aircraft has exited the wind shear condition.

What are the two types of wind shear conditions and how are they displayed?

The two types are increasing (caution) and decreasing performance (warning) windshear. Increasing performance is indicated by an amber wind shear presented on the PFD with the AMI and FD indicating 15 degrees.

During a decreasing performance windshear, a red WINDSHEAR warning is presented on the PFD along with an aural "windshear". The FD indicates 15 degrees and the AMI is presented at 30 degrees.

Explain the De-Clutter function.

During an unusual attitude all nonessential information is cleared from the PFD. The trip points for the de-clutter function are pitch angle in excess of +30 or -20 degrees, or roll in excess of 65 degrees. The only information presented is:

- Altitude

- Airspeed

- Attitude

- Vertical speed

- Compass

- Autopilot engage indicator

What occurs when the heading bug is selected off scale?

A dashed line appears from the center of the heading indicator to the bug and a digital heading indication will appear on the PFD.

What occurs when the heading or attitude information is invalid?

For heading information a red-boxed MAG, DG or TRUE will appear and the heading display is removed from the PFD. For attitude a red-boxed ATT appears and the attitude information is removed from the PFD.

If DME hold is on, will the FMS auto tune on that side?

No

How would you know if DME hold is activated?

An amber H replaces the NM of the navigation source indication on the PFD and the station identifier is removedThere is an amber "H" on the RTU next to the frequency.

Why is the station identifier removed from the navigation source indi-cation when DME hold is activated?

The data for the identifier is supplied by the DME.

How would you find all the VOR and DME stations in use by the FMS?

Bring up the VOR/DME STATUS page and this will list all of the stations in use.

How are the bearing indications displayed on the PFD?

The BRG switches on the DCP.

What bearing indications can be presented on the PFD?

- VOR 1, VOR 2

- ADF 1, ADF 2

- FMS 1, FMS 2 (FMS 2 only on dual FMS aircraft)

What is the distance of the lateral deviation scale of the HSI needle?

- Each dot equals 5 degrees in VOR.

- Each dot equals 1 degree in LOC.

- Each dot equals 5 NM in FMS.

What does an amber YD displayed on the upper left side of the attitude indicator indicate?

It indicates that both yaw dampers have been disengaged.

What does an amber boxed A or E on the attitude indicator indicate?

An A indicates that the FCC has detected an aileron out of trim condition. An E indicates the FCC has detected an elevator out of trim condition.

How is a display control panel (DCP) failure indicated?

A red-boxed DCP flag on the PFD and MFD indicates failure of a DCP.

What occurs if a display has an over temperature?

When an over temperature condition is sensed, a red DISPLAY TEMP message will appear on the display. At this point all information is removed from the display but will return when the display cools.

What is the source of time data for the UTC clock on the top of the MFD?

The time is provided by the pilot's clock and if that fails, it will be provided by the first officer's clock.

How is weather radar displayed on the MFD?

Turn the radar on and select the WX/TERR button on the DCP.

What is the purpose of the NAV SOURCE selector switch on the DCP?

Select the Nav Source to be displayed on the MFD. The selections available are:

- HSI

- NAV SECTOR

- FMS MAP

- FMS PLAN MAP

- RADAR

What is the purpose of the PUSH X-SIDE button on the DCP NAV SOURCE Selector knob?

The button allows for the selection of cross-side course information to be displayed when using the HSI and NAV sector formats.

Explain the purpose of the FMS plan map selection on the NAV SOURCE.

This map is used during flight plan set up and en route modifications. North will always be displayed at the top. Selection of the FMS legs page, the flight plan route can be verified using the up or down keys on the FMS.

What MFD formats can the radar be displayed on?

- Navaid sector map

- TCAS

- FMS map

What static system supplies the standby instruments?

The standby pitot static system (P3 and S3) supplies the standby instruments.

Is electrical power required to operate the standby instruments?

No electrical power is required to operate the standby instruments. However electrical power is required to operate the friction vibrator for the standby altimeter.

What is the navigation source for the standby attitude indicator localizer and glideslope?

The source is VHF navigation receiver 1 or the backup tuning unit. During normal operations the backup tuning unit will be in STBY and it will display what is selected in NAV and COM 1.

If electrical power is lost to the standby attitude system, how long is attitude information displayed?

For a minimum of 9 minutes.

How long will the power OFF flag be displayed on the standby attitude indicator after initial power is applied?

The flag will remain for approximately two minutes.

What four conditions will display the power OFF flag on the standby attitude indicator?

- When there is no output AC power from the internal inverter.

- Insufficient gyro speed.

- PULL TO CAGE knob in caged position.

- No input power signal.

What supplies the aircraft time information?

Original Style: The two pilot clocks with the Captains being the primary source.

GPS Style: Upon power up if there is a valid GPS signal the clocks will be automatically set. If there is not a GPS signal or there is a need manually override the GPS signal, then the pilots can set the clock.

chapter 11

Fuel System

What provides static and dynamic venting for the fuel tanks?

NACA vent scoops under the wings provide static and dynamic venting.

Where are the collector tanks located?

The two collector tanks are located in the center tank at a point that is lower than the left or right wing tanks.

What are the maximum fuel tank capacities?

	Pressure	Gravity
Left Wing	4760 lbs. (2159 kg)	4488 lbs. (2036 kg.)
Right Wing	4760 lbs. (2159 kg)	4488 lbs. (2036 kg.)
Center	4998 lbs. (2267 kg.)	4930 lbs. (2237 kg.)
Total	14518 lbs (6585 kg)	13906 lbs. (6309 kg)

Explain the construction of the wing fuel tanks.

The wing tanks are a wet wing design. A sealant is used to seal the tanks so this makes the wing the tank.

How is gravity defueling accomplished?

A gravity defueler adapter can be inserted into the fuel drain valves to accomplish gravity defueling.

How is fuel prevented from flowing to the wing tip during wing low maneuvers?

There are one-way flow valves in each wing tank that prevent the flow of fuel to the wing tip.

Explain the fuel vent system.

The NACA scoops have vent lines connected to the tanks to provide static and dynamic pressure. In flight the NACA vents will provide ram air pressure to maintain a positive pressure on the fuel in the tanks.

Static ventilation of the tanks during ground operations is provided through the NACA vents. They will also relieve pressure caused by fueling or thermal expansion. To prevent fuel from coming out of the NACA vent when the aircraft is being refueled, the NACA vent line drains the fuel trapped in the vent lines back into the center tank.

During climb you notice the total fuel in the center tank increase by 300 lbs, is this a problem?

This is not a problem. It is possible for fuel to flow to the center tank from the vent system during climb and cause the fuel quantity readings of the center tank to increase as high as 300 lbs.

What monitors and controls the operation of the fuel system?

A dual-channel fuel system computer.

Do both fuel computer channels operate at the same time?

One channel operates at a time. When the active channel fails, the standby channel will assume control.

Where is the temperature of the fuel measured?

- Left wing tank

- In the fuel line to each engine

Explain the general operation of ejector pumps.

Motive fuel flow must come from a source like the engine high-pressure fuel pump. This motive flow is passed through a venturi-shaped nozzle. The fuel exits the nozzle at an increased velocity that creates a low pressure. This low pressure creates a suction that draws fuel out of the tank.

What powers the fuel ejectors?

Motive flow from the engine high-pressure pump. High-pressure fuel flows through a venturi-shaped nozzle of the ejector, which creates a low pressure. This then draws fuel out of the tank by suction.

How is fuel transferred from the wing tanks to the collector tanks?

Fuel is transferred by scavenge ejectors. A scavenge ejector is located at the lowest inboard point of each wing tank.

How is fuel moved from the collector tank to the high pressure engine driven fuel pump?

There is one main ejector pump for each collector tank. Motive flow to operate the main ejector is provided by the high-pressure output of the engine driven fuel pump.

How are the boost pumps powered?

The boost pumps are DC powered.

What are the purposes of the electric fuel boost pumps?

- To transfer fuel from the collector tanks to the engines.

- As a backup to the main ejectors when the ejector fails.

- Provide fuel pressure during engine start.

143

Are the electric boost pumps required for engine start?

No, the engines will start without them.

When will the electric boost pumps operate with the L and R boost pump switch light selected?

Both pumps will operate when the fuel computer detects low fuel feed pressure in either feed manifold.

Which electric boost pump will operate with just DC power?

The left DC pump.

Explain the transfer ejectors?

There are two transfer ejectors located in the aft section of the center tank and perform the job of transferring fuel from the center tank to the wing tanks. Motive flow created by the high-pressure output of the main ejectors operates the transfer ejectors.

Explain the engine fuel shutoff valves (SOV).

The associated ENGINE FIRE PUSH switch light on the glare shield electrically controls the SOV. Their purpose is to stop the flow of fuel to the engines. This switch light is located on the emergency bus so it is always powered.

Where is the engine fuel temperature indication located?

On the FUEL synoptic page.

How is the fuel heated before it enters the engine?

The fuel is heated by a fuel/oil heat exchanger located on each engine. Hot engine oil passes through the heat exchanger to heat the fuel.

How many fuel filters are installed?

There is one fuel filter per engine.

What would happen if the fuel filter becomes contaminated?

An impending bypass switch monitors the filter for contamination. If a low fuel pressure is sensed, an EICAS message will alert the crew. The filter will then be bypassed to continue to provide fuel to the engine.

Explain the XFLOW/APU pump?

This DC powered pump is used to supply fuel to the APU from both wing tanks equally and perform cross flow operations. The pump is located in the aft portion of the center wing box in the main landing gear bay.

Explain the APU fuel shutoff valve (SOV).

The APU SOV is used to stop the flow of fuel to the APU. This SOV is opened and closed by the APU FIRE PUSH switch light or by the PWR FUEL switch light on the APU control panel.

Explain the APU negative gravity relief valve.

This is a spring-loaded valve, which allows pressurized fuel from the right engine fuel feed manifold to feed the APU during two conditions.

- The valve would open if the XFLOW/APU fuel pump fails.

- A negative gravity condition exists in flight.

This valve is not indicated on the fuel synoptic page. The negative gravity relief valve allows the APU/XFLOW pump to be deferred. The APU will start and run with just the operation of the main boost pumps to feed fuel to the APU negative gravity relief valve.

What are the two methods to cross flow fuel?

- Powered cross flow (automatic or manual)

- Gravity cross flow

Tip! View the switch lights on the flight deck fuel panel as two "V's". One "V" right side up and one "V" upside down. The right side up "V" will be the L and R BOOST PUMP and the XFLOW AUTO OVERRIDE switch lights. These switch lights control pumps. The upside down "V" is the L and R XFLOW valves and the GRAVIITY XFLOW switch lights. These switch lights control valves.

Explain the operation of the automatic powered cross flow.

Automatic cross flow operation is initiated when there is a fuel imbalance of more than 200 lbs. (91 kg) between the wing tanks. The XFLOW/APU pump is powered and fuel is taken from both wing tanks. The cross flow valve on the low quantity side will open to fill the low side to 50 lbs. (23kg.) above the other side. This operation is enabled when the system is not in manual mode.

Explain the manual powered cross flow operation.

This feature is used when the automatic powered cross flow does not respond to an imbalance. The pilot can select the XFLOW AUTO OVERRIDE switch light to MANUAL, which will inhibit the automatic powered cross flow system.

The L or R cross flow SOV switch light can be selected on the low tank side. Selecting this switch light will cause the XFLOW/APU pump to activate and the cross flow valve to open on the side selected. The pilot must turn off the cross flow by deselecting the L or R XFLOW AUTO OVERRIDE switch light once balance is achieved. This will cause the valve to close and the XFLOW/APU pump to turn off.

When will the FUEL IMBALANCE caution message appear on the EICAS?

When there is an imbalance of 800 lbs. (363 kg.) between the wing tanks.

Explain the gravity cross flow operation?

This operation is used when the power fuel cross flow does not correct the fuel imbalance or the XFLOW pump is inoperative. The pilot can manually select the GRAVITY XFLOW switch light to open the gravity cross flow SOV. Fuel will flow through the gravity manifold to achieve a balance. The aircraft can be side slipped to help the fuel transfer.

What happens when the GRAVITY/XFLOW switch light is pressed?

The gravity XFLOW SOV is opened, a white OPEN illuminates on switch light and EICAS displays a green GRAV XFLOW OPEN.

What does the amber FAIL light in the GRAVITY XFLOW switch light indicate?

The gravity XFLOW SOV is not in the commanded position.

What should the pilots do to transfer fuel from the center tank to the wing tanks?

This process is completely automatic. The transfer ejectors do the transfer of fuel from the center tank to the wing tanks. This process does require motive flow, which means the engines need to be running.

What EICAS messages are displayed when fuel is transferred from the center tank to the wing tanks?

There are no EICAS messages or indications.

What are the two methods of fueling?

The two methods are pressure and gravity fueling.

Explain the process of transferring fuel from the center tank to the wing tanks.

This process is automatic and controlled by the fuel system computer. Transfer begins when the fuel level in wing tank drops below 94% of its capacity and there is fuel in the center tank. The appropriate fuel transfer valve will open, motive flow from the engine feed manifold flows through the open valve to the transfer ejector, which will transfer fuel from the center tank to the appropriate wing tank.

When the respective wing tank is full, the transfer valve will close. When the wing is 94% full, with fuel in the center tank, the process starts over. This is the same process for both wing tanks.

How is defueling accomplished?

The two methods of defueling are suction and gravity. After attaching the single point adapter, the fuel control panel can be configured to apply suction to extract fuel. Gravity defuel is accomplished by fuel drain valves on the lowest point of each tank.

Where are the refueling/defueling operations controlled?

On the right side of the aircraft located near the wing root is a refuel/ defuel control panel. There is also an optional refuel/defuel control panel that can be installed behind the copilots seat. If one is installed it has priority over the external panel.

Explain how to refuel in the Auto Mode.

Select the total fuel quantity desired through the increase/decrease switch and then select the refuel start switch to ON. The fuel computer will direct the fuel to the appropriate tanks and stop fueling when the select amount is reached.

Explain how to refuel in the Manual Mode.

Fuel is directed to a tank by selecting open or closed the appropriate shutoff valve.

What is the limitation for takeoff if there is more than 500 lbs. (227 kg.) of fuel in the center tank?

The fuel quantity in each wing tank must be above 4400 lbs. (1995 kg).

How does the fuel computer stop fueling when the tank is full?

This is accomplished by high-level sensors, which will signal the fuel computer to close the appropriate tank refuel shutoff valve.

Why should you never remove the gravity filler caps if the wing tanks are full or fuel quantity is not know?

The caps are located below the maximum pressure refueling level and fuel could come out if opened.

Upon boarding an aircraft the fuel person says the fuel panel will not work and he needs to gravity refuel. What should you think about?

What is the current level of the fuel tanks. The caps are located below the maximum pressure refueling level, and if the aircraft is already fueled above this level, fuel could flow out when the cap is removed.

Don't forget about the MEL and calling maintenance, you now have a piece of equipment that is not working.

What information does the fuel computer gather to calculate the fuel weight in each tank?

The fuel computer gets information from the fuel system and aircraft attitude information from the AHRS to calculate fuel weight.

Explain how to manually measure the amount of fuel in the tanks?

Magnetic level indicators (MLI) are used to manually check the fuel amount in each tank. There is one MLI for the center tank and two for each wing tank.

To check the fuel level, release the measuring stick and let it drop. As the float magnet and the magnet on the stick come in line, the stick will stop. The uncorrected tank quantity is indicated on the stick. This indication is then corrected by referring to the two inclinometers mounted on circuit breaker panel 2 to determine aircraft roll and pitch deviation from level. Refer to FCOM volume 2 to correct the deviation.

When will the fuel total turn amber?

900 lbs. (408 kg)

When will the bulk fuel temperature in the left wing turn amber?

-40 degrees C and below.

When will the left or right fuel feed temperatures turn amber?

5 degrees C or less.

When will the center fuel tank quantity indicate green?

When the quantity is 10 lbs. (5 kg.) or more. Below this amount the indication will turn white.

When will the left or right wing tank fuel quantity turn amber?

The indications will turn amber when the total fuel quantity is 900 lbs. (408 kg.) or less. They will also turn amber when a fuel quantity imbalance of more than 800 lbs. (363 kg.) between the wing tanks.

chapter 12

Hydraulics

How many hydraulic systems does the CRJ have?

The CRJ has a total of 3 hydraulic systems, which are identified by system 1,2 and 3.

In general, what systems are powered by at least one hydraulic system?

- Primary and secondary flight controls

- Wheel brakes

- Landing gear

- Nose wheel steering

Which systems are powered by more than one hydraulic system?

The primary flight controls and flight spoilers are powered by more than one hydraulic system.

Which hydraulic pumps are engine driven?

Hydraulic system pumps 1A and 2A.

Which hydraulic pumps are electrically driven?

All backup pumps (B pumps) and the system 3A pump are all alternating current motor pumps. These are 1B, 2B, 3A, and 3B.

What is the color of Skydrol hydraulic fluid?

It is a purplish color and should not be touched, as it is highly corrosive.

Specifically what does hydraulic system 1 power?

- Rudder and elevator

- Flight spoilers

- Left aileron and spoileron

- Outboard ground spoilers

Specifically what does hydraulic system 2 power?

- Outboard brakes

- Inboard ground spoilers

- Main landing gear auxiliary actuators

- Flight spoilers

- Right aileron and spoileron

- Rudder and elevator

What is the normal PSI of the hydraulic systems?

3000 PSI

What is the only difference between hydraulic system 1 and 2 other than what they operate?

The reservoir capacities are different; system 2 is larger due to powering more equipment.

When do system 1A and 2A main hydraulic pumps operate?

Any time the respective engine is operating.

What three things determine when the backup B pumps for system 1 and 2 will operate?

- Cross-side engine-driven generator output

- Flap position

- Hydraulic switch position

If you have an engine failure, the opposite side hydraulic B pump will be inoperative, even if the switch is put in the ON position.

Explain the AUTO switch position of hydraulic system 1 and 2.

Hydraulic pumps 1B and 2B will operate when they are powered, the flaps are not at zero, and the generator on the opposite side engine is operating.

Will hydraulic pump 1B or 2B automatically start after an engine failure or hydraulic pump 1A or 2A failure?

No, the 1B or 2B hydraulic switch must be selected to ON.

Remember: The cross-side generator must be operating for the ON position of pump 1B or 2B to work. The logic behind this is that if an engine fails, the cross-side generator will be operating, so that means that engine is running and that hydraulic A pump is operating and the on position will not be needed. This prevents overloading of the electrical system.

Explain the ON position of system 1 and 2.

This is the manual mode to operate hydraulic system 1 and 2 pumps. It will turn pumps 1B and 2B on.

During flight, if you place hydraulic system 1B or 2B switch to ON, will the pumps operate?

The pump will operate if the respective bus is powered and the generator on the opposite side engine is operating.

If you select the 1B or 2B hydraulic switch to ON with the aircraft on the ground and the engines not operating, will the pumps operate?

Yes, a circuit will allow the pumps to operate on the ground with the engine-driven generators not operating.

When will hydraulic pump 1B or 2B be load shed?

When an engine driven generator fails, the opposite side hydraulic pump (1B or 2B) will be load shed.

How are the hydraulic shutoff valves closed?

The valves are shutoff by pressing the ENG FIRE PUSH switch light.

What is the job of the hydraulic accumulator?

The accumulator is used to store hydraulic pressure to satisfy the instantaneous demands of aircraft systems. It also dampens pressure surges within the system. It is charged with dry nitrogen.

How many hydraulic accumulators does the aircraft have?

There are a total of 5 accumulators, one for each hydraulic system and one for each brake.

How are hydraulic systems 1 and 2 cooled?

Because pumps 1A and 2A are within the engine nacelles and generate a lot of heat, the fluid needs to be cooled. The fluid is cooled by a hydraulic oil heat exchanger that is located in the aft equipment bay.

The air used by the heat exchanger for cooling is drawn in through the ram air scoop. The air is exhausted out the exit point on each side of the aft part of the fuselage and has a wire screen over the exhaust area.

While on the ground an electric fan inside the heat exchanger draws the air from the ram air scoop.

Why does hydraulic system 3A and 3B not need a cooling system?

They are not near a heat source. The lines also run through the fuel tanks.

Where are hydraulic system 3's main components located and what are they?

The main components are an accumulator, a reservoir and two AC pumps (3A, 3B). They are located in or near the main landing gear bay.

Which hydraulic system has the largest demand?

System 3

What components do hydraulic system 3 power?

- Left and right aileron

- Rudder and elevator

- Left and right spoileron

- Landing gear

- Nose wheel steering

- Inboard brakes

- Nose door

When does the 3A pump operate?

During normal operations it runs continuously and is selected on via an ON/OFF switch.

What determines when the hydraulic pump 3B operates?

* Hydraulic switch position

* Flap position

* Emergency power (ADG)

If pump 3A fails will 3B automatically take over?

Not automatically, but the pump can be manually turned on by selecting the 3B switch to ON.

When will the hydraulic pump 3B automatically energize?

When the ADG is deployed, pump 3B energizes to maintain hydraulic power to the primary flight controls.

When the flaps are not at zero and the bus is powered, the hydraulic 3B pump will operate.

Explain the AUTO position of the hydraulic pump 3B switch.

The pump will operate when the flaps are not at zero and its bus is powered.

What will happen to the 3B pump if the switch is in the OFF position in flight and the ADG deploys?

The 3B pump will operate because the emergency mode is independent of the 3B switch position.

While in flight with the hydraulic switches in AUTO and 3A in the ON position, what pumps are running when the flaps are extended from 0 degrees?

All pumps will be operating during normal operations.

On the hydraulic synoptic page, when will the reservoir quantity indicate green?

Green: >45% and <85%

When will the hydraulic system pressure indicate an amber caution range?

Less than 1800 PSI

Will the APU generator power hydraulic pump 1B or 2B with their switch in ON and the engine generators not operating?

Only while on the ground is the operation of pump 1B and 2B not dependent on cross-side engine generator operation. This allows tests to be completed.

When all hydraulic pressure is lost to the brakes, do you have any braking capability?

There will be enough pressure for six brake applications due to the accumulators.

What is the green range of the hydraulic system pressure?

1800 to 3200 PSI

While in cruise with the flaps up, what pumps are operating?

1A, 3A, 2A

chapter 13

Ice & Rain Protection

Which areas of the aircraft are anti-iced?

- Wing leading edges

- Engine cowls

- Air data probes

- Windshields and flight side windows

How does the Ice Detector detect conditions that could lead to ice accumulation?

The ice detectors extend into the air stream and vibrate at high frequency. When ice accumulates on the probe the frequency of the vibration is dampened and the microprocessor sends a signal to the DCU to display an EICAS ICE caution message. The ICE DET switch light on the ANTI-ICE control panel will also illuminate.

How will the ice detector know when the aircraft has exited ice conditions?

When in ice conditions, the ice detector electrically heats the probe for 5 seconds during each 60-second cycle. After heating the probe, if it does not accumulate any more ice, then the indication is removed.

What components does the ice detector system consist of?

The system consists of two microprocessors and a probe on each side of the aircraft. These two systems are independent of each other. When the microprocessor detects ice on the probe, a signal is sent to the data concentrator units (DCU) and an amber caution ICE EICAS msg. is displayed.

After the ice detector detects ice and the wing and cowl anti-ice systems are turned on, how does the ice warning change?

It changes from an amber ICE EICAS message to an advisory green ICE message.

What happens when the 14th stage isolation valve switch light is pressed?

The 14th stage isolation valve opens to allow both wings to be anti-iced from a single 14th stage bleed from one engine. For the valve to operate it requires bleed air and electric power. This means that the wing anti-ice must be selected on first for it to work.

Where do the wings and cowls get bleed air for anti-icing?

The 14th stage bleed air off the engines.

How is bleed air directed onto the wing leading edge?

Piccolo tubes direct hot bleed air onto the inner surface of the leading edges.

How does the bleed air exit after heating the wing leading edge?

The bleed air exits through louvers located under the wing leading edges.

What is the normal position of the 14th stage isolation valve?

Closed

What position would the left and right wing anti-icing pressure regulating valves be in if there was a loss of 14th stage pressure or electrical power?

The valves are spring-loaded to the closed position. The valves require both 14th stage pressure and electrical power to open.

What position would the left and right wing anti-icing shutoff valves be in if there was a loss of 14th stage pressure or electrical power?

The valves are spring-loaded to the closed position.

What happens when the WING ANTI-ICE switch is selected to NORM?

The anti-ice temperature controller modulates the wing anti-icing valves to maintain a constant wing leading edge temperature.

What happens when the WING ANTI-ICE switch is selected to STBY?

This allows the temperature controller to be bypassed in case of failure. The anti-icing valves are cycled open or closed by thermal switches to maintain the leading edges at a lower temperature than the normal mode.

What happens when there is a wing overheat condition?

Sensors along the wing anti-icing dusk will send a signal to the DCUs and then display a WING OVHT warning on the EICAS primary page. There will also be an aural "wing overheat" warning. The A/ICE synoptic page will indicate the duct location of the overheat condition.

What happens to the wing anti-ice system during activation of the thrust reverse?

Anytime the thrust reversers are activated on the ground and the wing anti-ice system is selected in NORM or STBY, the wing anti-icing valves will close.

This allows all 14th stage bleed air to open the thrust reverse system. The wing anti-ice system will resume normal operation upon stowing the thrust reversers. The cowl anti-ice system will continue to work at all times during thrust reverser use.

What is the purpose of the 14th stage isolation valve switch light?

This valve allows both wings to be anti-iced from a single 14th stage engine source.

Is the 14th stage isolation valve normally open or closed during normal operations?

Closed

When would you open the 14th stage isolation valve?

When an engine is not capable of providing 14th stage bleed air like during an engine failure or the wing anti-icing valve fails.

What is needed to open the 14th stage isolation valve?

The valve is pneumatically operated and electrically controlled. Because the isolation valve is located downstream of the wing anti-icing valves, at least one of the wing anti-icing valves must be open to supply the bleed air needed to open. Both air and electric is required.

What position does the 14th stage isolation valve fail?

The valve is spring loaded closed, if there is a loss of electrical control power or 14th stage bleed air pressure the valve will close.

If there is an engine failure, will the 14th stage isolation valve still operate?

Yes, there is electrical power and 14th stage bleed air on one side of the isolation valve when the wing anti-ice is selected.

Is the engine nose cone anti-iced?

Yes, by engine oil.

What part of the engine is anti-iced and by what source?

The leading edge of the cowl and the T2 sensor on each engine is anti-iced by 14th stage bleed air. The nose cone is anti-iced by engine oil.

Where does the 14th stage bleed exit after anti-icing the cowl and T2 probe?

The bleed air discharges into the atmosphere through louvers on the underside of the engine nacelle.

Which position will the cowl anti-ice valves fail?

The valves fail in the open position.

How is overpressure protection provided for the cowl anti-ice?

A pressure relief valve on each engine provides overpressure protection. The relief valve will extend, venting 14th stage air overboard. This valve is located on the underside of the engine and is visible during the walk around. It will require maintenance to return the valve to the normal position.

What normally reduces the high 14th stage bleed air to a level usable for cowl anti-icing?

The cowl anti-icing valves reduce the 14th stage bleed air.

What would happen if a cowl anti-icing valve failed to reduce the 14th stage bleed air pressure?

The pressure relief valve would extend to relieve the pressure.

The cowl anti-icing valves and the wing anti-icing valves are called CMD valves. What does this mean?

This is the position commanded by the switch and does not mean actual position of the valve. The valves are indicated on the ANTI-ICE page.

What provides control and monitoring of the probe and sensor heating?

There are three separate air data sensor heater controllers (ADSHC) that provide control and monitoring.

How many heaters are in a pitot static probe?

There are two heaters in each probe. There is one in the base and another in the head.

Explain the different heating modes of the pitot static probes in respect to head and base heating?

The head heater will operate at half heat on the ground and full heat in flight. The base heater operates at full heat in flight only.

Explain the heating of the standby pitot probe?

When turned on, it is provided half power for heating on the ground and full power in flight.

Where is the standby pitot probe located?

It is located on the left side of the nose.

Where are the alternate static ports located?

The alternate static ports are on each side of the aircraft towards the front.

Are the alternate static ports heated to full heat or half heat on the ground?

When selecting the probe switches to ON, it energizes the alternate static ports at full heat.

Where are the angle of attack (AOA) vanes located?

Located on each side of the aircraft below the cockpit windows.

When energized, what level of heating are the AOA vanes provided?

The AOA vanes are heated to full power on the ground or in flight. The probe switches activate this function.

Where is the total air temperature (TAT) located?

On the right side of the aircraft near the flight deck window.

When is the TAT probe heated and to what level?

It is heated at full heat in flight only. Regardless of the probe switches, the TAT is not heated on the ground.

Explain the ground mode of the air data sensor controllers (ADSHC).

While on the ground with one generator supplying power and the probe switches are in the OFF position, the ADSHC will apply half power to the three pitot heads only.

When the pilot selects the probe heater to ON, the ADSHC will then apply full power to the standby static ports and AOA sensors in addition to half power to the three pitot heads that were already powered. The TAT and pitot bases are not heated on the ground regardless of probe switch positions.

Explain the flight mode of the ADSHC computers.

When the aircraft is weight-off-wheels, the ADSHC's will apply full heat to all probe heaters regardless of probe or generator switch position.

What would happen if an ADSHC lost power?

All probes connected to that ADSHC would revert to full power.

Are any of the ADSHCs applying power to the probes or sensors when the aircraft is at the gate with just external power or APU power and the probe switches in the OFF position? What if the probes switches are selected ON?

In the OFF position nothing is being powered. With the switches selected ON, the ADSHC's will apply half power to the three pitot heads, full power to the standby static ports and angle of attack sensors. The TAT and pitot bases are not heated on the ground.

How do the flight deck windshields maintain a constant temperature?

There are four temperature controllers, one for each window, that monitor the electrical resistance of the temperature sensors in the glass. The power to the windshields is cycled on and off to maintain a certain glass temperature. A coating applied to inner surface of the outer glass panel is supplied electrical power for windshield heating.

Are the side cockpit windows anti-iced?

The side windows are de-fogged/de-misted only. They operate on one temperature schedule.

Are the forward flight deck windshields anti-iced?

Yes, anti-iced and also de-fogged/de-misted.

What windows does the LH WSHLD switch control?

It controls the left window and left windshield.

When the LH or RH WSHLD switch is placed in LOW, what happens?

The warm-up cycle begins to prevent thermal shock to the windshields and windows. After the warm-up cycle, the temperature controllers maintain a low heat level.

What would happen if a windshield or window started to overheat?

The overheat protection would remove power from the affected surface.

After a window or windshield overheat condition, how could the temperature controller be reset?

Move the WSHLD switch to the OFF/RESET position will de-energize the windshield and window on that side and reset the temperature controller.

When would you use the WSHLD HI position?

Only when LOW does not do the job.

Will the windshield test work when the WSHLD switches are in the OFF position?

No

How is the windshield and window system test completed?

The WSHLD switches should be in LOW or HI and then press and hold the TEST switch. The test passes when an amber L and R WSHLD HEAT and L and R WINDOW HEAT caution messages appear on the EICAS.

Explain the wing overheat test.

Press the wing OVHT/DUCT FAIL switch light. A good test is indicated by a WING A/ICE OK advisory message, an OVHT EICAS warning message, an aural "wing overheat" and the OVHT will illuminate in the switch light.

What does the OVHT and the DUCT FAIL light in the WING switch light on the ANTI-ICE panel indicate?

OVHT - When there is a overheat condition in the wing leading edge this light will illuminate.

DUCT FAIL - When there is a bleed air leak detected in the left or right wing anti-ice ducts this light will illuminate.

Explain the ICE DET TEST switch light on the ANTI-ICE panel.

When pressed, the ice detector circuitry and probes are tested. A good test is indicated by illumination of the DET TEST switch light and a caution ICE message on the EICAS if the temperature of the wing is below 18 degrees C. If the temperature of the wing is above 18 degrees C then a green advisory EICAS ICE message will be displayed.

Explain the STBY position of the WING ANTI-ICE switch.

The wing temperature controller is bypassed and the wing anti-ice valves cycle open and closed at a predetermined temperature. This temperature is cooler than the NORM position.

If the copilot has the windshield wiper selected to LOW and the captain then selects HI, who has control?

The captain will then have control and the wipers will move at HI speed. If the captain then selects OFF, the wipers will move at LOW speed and the copilot will then have control.

What does an amber wing anti-ice duct on the ANTI-ICE synoptic page indicate?

Low duct pressure or low temperature. This will also be associated with an EICAS L/R WING A/ICE message.

What does a green ICE on the EICAS indicate during flight?

Ice is detected and the anti-ice system is operational with sufficient heat and pressure.

chapter 14

Indicating & Recording [EICAS]

In what order are the messages displayed on the crew alerting system (CAS)?

The messages are prioritized by importance and occurrence.

How does the pilot know what message is the most recent on the CAS?

The most recent message is at the top of the associated list (ex. abnormal or warning).

What are the four levels of CAS messages?

- Warning

- Caution

- Advisory

- Status

How are the CRTs powered, DC or AC powered?

DC

Are the CRTs cooling fans DC or AC powered?

AC

How many CRT cooling fans does the aircraft have?

3

Do all the CRT cooling fans operate at the same time?

No, the fan that operates is determined by the proximity sensing system (PSS). The DSPLY FAN knob on the DISPLAY FAN and ARINC FAN control panel can be used to select different fans.

With just the battery master on, what limitation do you need to be aware of?

Because the CRT display fans are AC powered, the fans are not operating with just the battery master on. The limitation is 5 minutes due to no cooling airflow for the CRTs.

What is the main component responsible for getting the information to the EICAS?

The two data concentrator units (DCU). The DCUs receive information from many aircraft systems, process the information and relays it to the proper component or display.

Explain the Lamp Driver Unit (LDU).

This unit controls the panel and glare shield switch light illumination. The LDU has two-channels for redundancy, should one channel fail the other will continue to operate. When the DCU sends a message to the EICAS the message is also sent to the LDU, which then will illuminate the appropriate switch light.

How do you test the LDU?

The LAMP TEST switch on the miscellaneous test panel does the LDU test. Place the switch in 1 or 2 and this will test the associated LDU and panel lamps. This will illuminate most lights.

For LAMP TEST 1 the FCC lights to the left of each button on the FCP will illuminate and not the right side light. The right side will illuminate with LAMP TEST 2. The DCU light on the First Officers side panel will illuminate with the associated LAMP TEST (ex. LAMP TEST 1 will illuminate DCU 1).

How is the lamp light intensity set to bright or dim?

The IND LTS switch on the miscellaneous test panel sets lamp intensity.

What always accompanies the master warning?

A triple chime aural warning always accompanies the master warning.

What may also accompany a master warning?

A voice message or a dedicated tone.

How can a flashing master warning switch light and the audio alert be cancelled?

By pressing the master warning switch light.

What always accompanies a master caution switch light?

A single chime.

What does the AURAL WARN TEST switch do?

This switch is located on the miscellaneous test panel and is used to test the audio outputs of the DCUs. Position 1 tests DCU 1 and position 2 tests DCU 2. Positioning the switch in 1 or 2 will begin the test for that respective DCU and voice warnings are sounded sequentially. To interrupt the test, select the test position again.

How could you disable the aural warnings of a particular DCU?

On the copilot's side panel there are two (optional third) AUDIO WARNING DISABLE switch lights. These switch lights are use to disable and silence the aural warnings of a DCU. When one DCU is disabled the other will provide aural warnings. If all DCUs are disabled, all EICAS aural warnings are disabled.

Are the GPWS and TCAS aural warnings disabled by selecting the AUDIO WARNING disable switches on the copilot's side panel?

No

Which four buttons on the EICAS Control Panel (ECP) will still operate if the ECP microprocessor fails?

- PRI

- CAS

- STAT

- STEP

Is there a backup to the microprocessor for the ECP?

No, there is just one processor for the ECP.

Explain the PRI button on the ECP.

The primary page will be displayed on ED2.

Explain the STAT button on the ECP.

The status page will be displayed on ED2. Pressing the button after the status page is on ED2 will cause the status messages to be removed and replaced by a white MSGS icon. If the DCU generates a new status message, the status messages will reappear with the new message at the top.

Can the CAS messages be cleared?

By pressing the CAS button while in flight or on the ground with the engines running, the caution messages will be replaced by an amber MSGS icon. You cannot box CAS caution messages on the ground with the engines not running or a single engine running.

How can all the synoptic pages on ED2 be viewed during an ECP failure?

The STEP button will view the pages in order from left to right as displayed on the ECP panel.

What is the function of the MENU button on the ECP?

- The N1 reference can be set to display on the primary page.

- The fuel used can be reset.

When will the SEL, UPD and DN button on the ECP work?

Only when the MENU page is selected.

Why are the N1 fan vibration gauges not displayed right after engine start?

Once *both* engines are stabilized at idle and engine oil pressures are in the normal range, the N1 fan vibration gauges replace the oil pressure gauges. The oil pressure gauges will return upon engine shut down.

Does the N2 section of the engine have a vibration indication?

The N2 VIB gauge will be displayed on the N2 gauge when vibration exceeds a certain value.

What indications can be displayed on the N1 gauges?

- APR

- REV

- Thrust setting

Only when the systems are activated.

During flight when will the landing gear and flap position display be removed?

When all of the following are met:

- The wheel brake temperatures are in the normal range.

- Landing gear is up and locked.

- Flaps are up.

The gear and flap position indication will be displayed again when either is selected.

What types of messages are presented on ED2?

Status and advisory messages.

What types of messages are presented on ED1?

Warning and caution messages are presented on ED1.

When will the APU RPM and EGT gauge be displayed?

When the APU PWR FUEL switch light is selected.

When is the APU door position indication displayed?

It is displayed continuously on ED2.

When will the crew oxygen display on ED2 turn amber to indicate a low quantity?

1410 PSI

During flight when will the brake temperature indicators be removed from display on ED2?

When all 3 conditions are met:

- Landing gear is up and locked

- All brake temperatures are normal

- Flaps are up

How is the DC ELEC synoptic page displayed?

By pressing the ELEC button on the ECP two times.

When would you most likely use the MENU page on the ECP?

Most aircraft are equipped so the outside air temperature can be set into the FMS and proper N1 takeoff power settings will be displayed. If the FMS fails, the power settings for takeoff and go around will need to be set. The fuel used will also need to be reset via the MENU page. All of this is done on the MENU page.

What does the magenta color indicate for the EICAS color logic?

Insufficient data to determine proper color-coding.

What does a light shade of cyan color indicate in reference to the EICAS color logic?

The component is operational.

Explain the color logic of the valves on the synoptic pages.

The valve is white if it is operable and amber if it is inoperable. The exception is the wing anti-ice and cowl valves. The A/ICE page does not indicate the actual position but shows the commanded position (CMD) of the control switches. This is why the valve is a cyan color.

Explain the color logic of the fuel and hydraulic pumps on their respective synoptic page.

- White - off

- Green - operating

- Amber - failed

What always accompanies a warning message?

- Flashing master warning lights on the glare shield panel.

- Triple chime.

- The switch associated with the system may have a red light <u>or</u>,

- A red indication on the EFIS <u>or</u>,

- A red indication on the synoptic page.

- Or some of these together.

What will sometimes accompany a warning message?

One or both of the following:

- Aural warning tone

- Voice message

When there is a warning message, what three things happen when either master warning switch light is pressed?

- Stops the master warning lights from flashing.

- Silences the aural alerts.

Will a caution message be displayed above a warning message?

No, caution messages will always be displayed below any warning messages displayed on the CAS.

What always accompanies a caution message?

- Flashing master caution lights.

- Single chime.

- The EFIS will have an amber indication, <u>and or</u>

- The faulted switch will have an amber light, <u>and or</u>

- The associated synoptic page will have an amber indication.

What happens when there is a master caution message and a master caution switch light is pressed?

- Resets the CAS to allow it to annunciate another fault.

- Cancels the flashing master caution lights.

If there is more than one page of caution messages on the CAS, how are they all viewed?

Pressing the CAS button it will cycle the pages.

Can an advisory message be cleared like the caution messages?

No, green advisory messages can only be cleared by deselecting the switch that created it.

What do the green advisory messages advise the crew of?

- Successful system test

- Aircraft configuration

- SOV closure

Where are the white status messages presented?

On the status page directly below the advisory messages if present.

What do the white status messages inform the crew of?

- When a system has been automatically or manually activated it indicates the status of the system.

- Failure of a low priority system.

How can more than one page of status messages be viewed?

By pressing the STAT button on the ECP.

Can the status messages be cleared from view?

Pressing the STAT button a second time can clear the status messages. A white-boxed MSGS icon will take their place.

Explain the phases of flight that the DCU inhibits distracting EICAS messages?

Takeoff:

- Condition 1: N1 greater that 79% and less than 100 KTS.

- Condition 2: Greater than 100 KTS.

Landing:

- Condition 3: Less than 400 feet AGL and will last until 30 seconds after touch down or greater than 400 feet on go-around.

What is the purpose of the EICAS reversionary mode?

It provides an alternate method of displaying EICAS information when ED1 or ED2 fail. It basically controls what is presented on the multi-function display (MFD). PFD or EICAS can be displayed.

What happens if ED1 fails?

The primary page automatically is transferred to ED2.

What happens if ED2 fails?

There is no automatic transfer of ED2. The pilot can use the EICAS switch on the Display Reversionary Panel (DRP) to display the STATUS page from ED2 on the MFD.

What condition will cause the ECP to be inactive?

Automatic transfer of the primary page to ED2 or failure of ED2.

Where are the display reversionary panels (DRP) and what do they do?

The DRP is located on the pilot and copilot side panel. They control the presentation of the PFD or EICAS on the associated multi function display (MFD).

Explain the EICAS switch position on the DRP.

The STATUS page will be displayed on the associated MFD and the ECP will now function.

Explain the PFD position on the DRP.

If the primary flight display (PFD) fails, the PFD information can be displayed on the associated MFD.

Explain the EICAS selector on the source selection panel.

There are three positions NORM, ED1 and ED2. This knob is used if either EICAS display fails, which will allow all EICAS information to be presented on the operative ED.

- NORM - normal EICAS displays.

- ED1 - if ED2 fails this will allow all EICAS information to be viewed on ED1 and the ECP is now fully functional.

- ED2 - if ED1 fails this will allow all EICAS information to be viewed on ED2 and the ECP is now fully functional.

What would happen if ED1 was the only operative ED with ED1 selected on the source selection panel and a warning message is generated?

If ED1 were displaying a synoptic, status or menu page it would revert back to the primary page automatically.

Is there a reversionary mode for the normal information displayed on the MFD?

No

What would you do if a MFD was displaying a maintenance menu when you boarded an aircraft with no maintenance being done?

The red guarded switch on circuit breaker panel was probably accidentally turned on.

When does the flight data recorder (FDR) start recording?

When the strobe lights or beacon are turned on. It is also activated by the Proximity Sensing System's weight off wheels switches.

Explain the FDR EVENT button on the miscellaneous test panel.

When pressed, it marks a significant event on the FDR.

How will the FMS get the time if GPS is not available and the aircraft is equipped with a GPS clock?

The captain's clock will be primary and the FO's clock is secondary. The pilot will have to manually set the time and this will disable the GPS clock function.

What components of the aircraft does the left side clock provide time to?

- ARINC bus

- FDR

- DCUs

Upon pushback and starting the engines a white FDR FAIL status msg. appears. What would you do?

Turn on the beacon switch; it is probably not on.

chapter 15

Landing Gear

What hydraulic system powers the landing gear?

Hydraulic system number 3 powers the landing gear.

Which hydraulic system powers the nose wheel steering?

Hydraulic system number 3 powers the nose wheel steering.

What is the job of the proximity sensing system (PSS)?

This is the system that consists of proximity sensors, proximity sensing electronic unit (PSEU), proximity switches and micro switches. The PSS monitors the aircraft doors, ground spoilers, thrust levers, parking brake, flap position and sequences the landing gear.

What does the PSEU monitor on the landing gear?

The nose doors, position of the landing gear, up locks and down locks.

What happens to the nose wheel steering and the anti-skid after takeoff?

The PSEU disables the nose wheel steering and anti-skid systems.

What activates the nose wheel steering and anti-skid systems upon landing?

PSEU

What happens if a main landing gear or a nose landing gear proximity sensor fails?

Each gear has dual proximity sensors; the other one will still function.

What powers the forward nose gear doors?

Hydraulic system #3 powers the nose gear doors.

What provides the shock absorption for the main landing and nose gear?

They are nitrogen-charged and oil filled.

How is the main landing gear and nose gear held in the up position?

By mechanical up locks.

How is the main landing gear held in the down position?

The strut actuators have locking mechanisms that lock the gear in the down position.

What closes the main landing gear doors?

The doors are attached to the main landing gear struts so the gear pulls the doors shut.

What is the purpose of the brush seals on the main landing gear doors and wheel bins?

They provide an aerodynamic seal.

How is the nose gear held in the down position?

The nose gear is held in the down position by an over-center locking mechanism.

When the nose gear is down and locked, are the gear doors opened or closed?

Closed

How do you open the nose gear doors from outside the cockpit?

On the external service panel there is a switch for ground operations. Hydraulic system #3 must be on.

Why should you use caution when turning on the hydraulic system #3 while on the ground?

If the doors are open and the external service panel nose door switch is in the close position, the doors would close and someone in the nose gear bay could get hurt.

What is the general process of operation when the landing gear lever is selected to the up or down position?

The PSS receives the signal from the landing gear lever; it looks landing gear proximity sensors and weight-on-wheel function. If all the proper conditions are met, the PSEU will signal the selector valves to retract or extend the landing gear.

What is the maximum gear retraction speed?

200 KIAS

Are the main landing gear wheels stopped after liftoff?

Yes, hydraulic pressure is applied to the wheel brakes.

Can you raise the landing gear lever while on the ground?

No, a solenoid lock prevents this. At weight-off-wheels on takeoff, the PSS removes the solenoid lock so the gear could be selected up.

What would you do if on takeoff the landing gear lever would not go up?

This would occur if the solenoid lock or PSS malfunctioned. Use the down lock release button next to the gear handle to manually override the solenoid lock.

What is the maximum speed to extend the landing gear?

250 KIAS

What are the possible causes if the landing gear will not extend?

Hydraulic system #3 has failed or there is a problem with the landing gear control circuitry.

How would you extend the landing gear if normal operation failed?

Refer to the checklist. The manual landing gear release handle can be used to lower the gear. When pulled it releases the all three landing gear up-locks and the up-locks for the forward nose gear doors.

During manual landing gear extension, how is the landing gear put in the down and lock position?

After the up locks are released the nose gear pushes the nose doors open. The nose gear is locked down by the airflow and by two over-center springs. The main landing gear is assisted by free-fall and by the main landing gear auxiliary actuators (MLG AUX ACT).

What powers the main landing gear auxiliary actuators during manual gear extension?

Hydraulic system #2

After manual gear extension, do you stow the handle?

The handle is pressed and lowered to the stow position.

Explain the overheat detection in the main landing gear bay?

The system consists of a single heat-sensing loop the runs through the MLG wheel bin. The system has a dual channel overheat detection unit. The overheat warnings and system faults are displayed on the EICAS. The system continuously monitors the MLG wheel bins for overheat conditions.

Explain the main landing gear bay overheat test?

The OVHT TEST simulates an overheat condition in the system. This test displays a red EICAS warning MLG BAY OVHT and creates an aural "gear bay overheat". When the OVHT TEST WARN FAIL switch is tested it simulates a failure of the MLG bay overheat detection system and displays an amber EICAS MLG OVHT FAIL caution message.

How is nose wheel steering accomplished?

By the steering tiller to 70 degrees either side or by the rudder pedals to 5 degrees either side.

How is the nose wheel moved by the controls?

The hydraulic system #3 moves the nose wheel. Nose wheel steering commands are transmitted by a "steer-by wire" system.

How is the nose wheel centered on take off?

On takeoff the nose wheel is centered by centering cams as the oleo extends.

Can a nose wheel steering fault be detected in flight?

Yes, the system is continuously monitored.

How far will the nose wheel move when the NWS is disarmed?

It free castors to 70 degrees either side.

What is the purpose of the rings on the outside of the nose tires?

These are called chine tires and are used to eject water off the ground away from the engines.

What is the speed limitation for the tires?

182 KIAS ground speed is the speed limit.

Which hydraulic systems power the brakes?

The outboard brakes are powered by hydraulic system #2 and the inboard brakes are powered by hydraulic system #3.

How are the tires protected against an overheated wheel or brake?

The main wheels have four fusible plugs in each tire. If the tire is overheated, the plugs melt and the tire deflates to prevent the tire form bursting.

How is brake temperature monitored?

By the brake temperature monitoring system (BTMS).

How are the main wheels stopped after liftoff?

When the gear is retracted, hydraulic pressure from the nose gear is directed to the main wheel brakes to stop rotation.

Why are the main wheels stopped before gear retraction on takeoff?

This will stop the gyroscopic precession.

Would you have any braking ability if hydraulic system 2 and 3 fail?

If hydraulic system #2 or #3 or both fail, each system has an accumulator that provides enough pressure for six brake applications. The anti-skid has to be selected off to have these six brake applications.

There is a loss of 50% in braking when one system fails and anti-skid is available on the side that is working.

When should the brakes be serviced?

When the brake wear indicator pins are flush with the top of the indicator housing. Hydraulic system #2 and #3 must be on and the brakes applied for an accurate check of the pins. If the parking brake is on, this counts as the brakes applied.

How do you set the parking brake?

Press the toe brakes on both pedals and pull the parking brake.

What hydraulic systems have to be on for the parking brake to hold?

Hydraulic systems #2 (powers outboard brakes) and #3 (powers inboard brakes).

Does the parking brake hold when the hydraulic systems #2 and #3 are turned off?

The inboard brakes will hold for an extended period of time.

In general how does the anti-skid work?

The speed of the tire and its speed of deceleration are sensed by the wheel speed transducers. This information is sent to the Anti-Skid Control Unit (ASCU) and it controls the hydraulic pressure to the brake to prevent lockup.

Explain how the anti-skid compares the speed of paired wheels?

The outboard wheel of each main gear is a pair and the inboard wheel of each main gear is a pair. If the outboard wheel of the left main rotates at a slower speed then the outboard of the right main, the anti-skid control unit releases the slower turning wheel brake. When the paired wheels reach the same speed, the brake will be reapplied.

What is the purpose of the ARMED switch on the anti-skid control panel?

This arms the anti-skid system when both main landing gear are down and locked and the parking brake is not applied.

What does the anti-skid system do when the aircraft becomes airborne?

The anti-skid control unit opens the anti-skid valves to full open to prevent wheel lock-up at touchdown.

When does the anti-skid system become operational upon landing?

At 35 knots wheel speed or after weight-on-wheels of 5 seconds, the anti-skid system becomes operational.

What is the minimum speed the anti-skid is operational?

10 knots, below this it does not operate.

Explain the anti-skid test.

The parking brake must be off and the test is accomplished by the selection of the anti-skid test switch on the ANTI SKID control panel. This test will simulate a failure in both anti-skid channels. Failure of the test is when one or both of the amber A/SKID INBD or A/SKID OUTBD messages are still present after the test.

What is the number range of the brake temperature monitoring system (BTMS)?

0 to 20

What is the equivalent temperature change for one unit of the BTMS?

One unit equals approximately 35 degrees C (95 F).

What values does the BTMS numbers change color?

- 0-5 green

- 6-11 white

- 12-20 red

Explain the BTMS overheat reset button.

If the BTMS system reaches the red zone, the BTMS will not reset the red brake reading even after the brake cools. The reset button must be pressed to reset the system. If the brake is still overheated, it will not reset when the button is pressed.

Maintenance should be contacted before resetting the system.

What must be done if the BTMS system has a value greater than 5?

Consult QRH Vol. 1 to determine brake-cooling requirements.

Explain the process of determining brake cooling time requirements when there is a 5 or greater.

Refer to your QRH or POH for the procedure. Use the brake cooling charts using the V1/V1mbe ratio.

What does the landing configuration warning system monitor?

The warning system monitors:

- Thrust lever position

- Airspeed

- Flaps

- Landing gear lever position

When can the landing gear warning horn be muted?

There are two conditions that the horn can be muted:

- Less than 185 KIAS, flaps 0 and one thrust lever at idle.

- Less than 163 KIAS, flaps 5-30 and one thrust lever at idle.

When would a "Too Low Gear" aural warning be heard?

When any of the 3 landing gear is not down and locked, the IAS is less than 190 KIAS and the radio altimeter reads less than 500 feet AGL.

When is the landing gear warning horn automatically inhibited?

On takeoff for two minutes after weight-off-wheels. Also on takeoff with wind shear present.

After takeoff when will the EICAS BTMS, gear and flaps indications be removed?

30 seconds after weight off wheels and the following conditions are met:

- Flaps are up

- BTMS indications are normal

- Landing gear is up and locked

chapter 16

Lighting

Where are the strobe lights located?

One in each wing tip and one in the tail cone.

What lights will turn on the flight data recorder?

When the strobe or beacon switch is turned on.

What lights do the RECOG/TAXI LTS switch control?

This switch controls the recognition and taxi light in the wing roots. This is one light in each wing root used for taxi purposes and makes it more visible in flight.

What lights do the left and right landing light switch control?

This will turn on the landing light and taxi-recognition light in the wing root for that side.

What lights do the NOSE landing light switch turn on?

The two landing lights in the nose.

How are the ceiling and sidewall fluorescent lights in the cabin controlled?

The CEILING and SIDEWALL switches on the flight attendant's panel.

How is the floodlighting at the forward entrance controlled?

The DOME switch on the flight attendant's panel controls them.

What lights does the BOARDING LIGHTS switch on the flight attendant's panel control?

In the ON position the boarding lights are at low intensity. When in the ON position the BRT switch is armed and if selected, the boarding lights will be in high intensity and the stair light will be illuminated.

What does the reading light TEST switch do?

All reading lights will be illuminated.

Explain the AUTO position of the NO SMKG and SEAT BELTS switches on the PASS SIGNS control panel on the flight deck.

In AUTO three things control position the illumination of the signs:

- Flap position

- Gear position

- Cabin altitude

When the flaps are extended out of 0 degrees, the seat belt sign will illuminate. Both signs will illuminate when the gear is extended. When the cabin altitude exceeds 10,000 feet, both signs will illuminate.

What controls the activation of the seat belt signs and no smoking signs when cabin altitude exceeds 10,000 feet?

The cabin pressure acquisition module (CPAM). The NO SMKG and SEAT BELTS switches must be in AUTO.

Where are service compartment lights located?

- Avionics bay

- Aft equipment bay

- Cargo bay

- Nose gear wheel well

Would the aircraft batteries be drained if a service compartment light were left on after the aircraft was shut down?

The lights don't work without power on the aircraft.

How are the emergency lights powered?

The emergency lights are powered by four rechargeable batteries.

How long will the batteries supply power to the emergency lights?

15 minutes

How are the emergency lights controlled?

There is an EMER LTS switch on the overhead panel of the flight deck. Also there is an EMERG LIGHT switch on the flight attendant's panel.

Which switch overrides the other emergency light switch?

The flight attendants switch will override the flight decks switch if it is in the off position.

With the emergency light switch in the ARM position, when will the emergency lights illuminate?

When all essential DC or essential AC power is lost.

How many emergency lights are over the wing?

There are three emergency lights over each wing.

What lights come on if only the left landing light is selected on?

The left landing light and the left recog/taxi light.

chapter 17

Navigation

What are the different methods of tuning the radios, navigation and transponders?

- Radio tuning unit (RTU)

- FMS radio page

- Standby radio

How many DME signals is the VHF NAV system capable of receiving?

The two VHF NAV receivers can receive up to three channels each for a total of six channels.

When will the FMS not auto-tune the VHF NAV receiver?

- When NAV SOURCE is not the FMS.

- When the DME HOLD is selected on the RTU.

- If the FMS Tune Inhibit switch is activated.

Where are the two DME antennas located?

They are just forward of the wing leading edge on the bottom of the aircraft.

Where are the marker beacon antennas located?

The antennas are just forward of the aft equipment bay door on the bottom of the fuselage.

How would you access the main page of the RTU?

Press the selected line key twice.

When using DME hold, what DME channel does it use?

The #2 DME channel.

What are the indications that the VHF NAV is in DME hold?

- An amber H replaces the NM on the PFD and MFD. The station identifier is also removed.

- On the RTU main page an amber H is next to the DME frequency.

- On the RTU top page there is an amber H below the active frequency.

How will you know if the VOR or ADF is not receiving a signal from the station by looking at the bearing pointers on the PFD or MFD?

The bearing pointers will not be visible.

How many transponders are installed?

2

What are the different modes of the transponders?

- Mode A – reports aircraft identity only.

- Mode C – reports aircraft altitude.

- Mode S – communicates with other mode C and S transponders for the TCAS.

Where are the antennas for the transponders?

There are two antennas for each transponder, one on the upper forward fuselage and one lower forward fuselage for each transponder.

Explain transponder mode S.

The ATC data link capability is used to communicate with other mode C and S transponder equipped aircraft to provide TCAS protection. This means that one aircraft's TCAS will tell the pilots to climb while the other aircrafts TCAS will tell it to descend. The transponder sends altitude data from the on-side ADC when interrogated.

Explain transponder mode C.

The transponder sends altitude data from the on-side ADC when interrogated.

What would happen if the transponder requests on-side altitude data from the on-side ADC, but it has failed?

The cross-side ADC data will be sent to the transponder by the RTU.

Explain transponder mode A.

When the transponder is interrogated it replies with an identification code.

Transponder 2 uses which ADC?

ADC 2

What is the purpose of the Enhanced Ground Proximity Warning System (EGPWS)?

The EGPWS helps prevent controlled flight into terrain (CFIT) and provides warning of severe wind shear.

What are the features of the EGPWS?

- Mode 1-5 which is the basic GPWS.

- Excessive bank angle alert and altitude callouts, which is mode 6.

- Wind shear detection and alerts, which is mode 7.

- Obstacle databases and terrain clearance floor on the MFD.

Explain the terrain clearance floor database (TCF) of the EGPWS.

This provides worldwide coverage of all airports with runways 3500 feet or longer. This feature has a protection zone around the airport that is based on the distance from the runway. The protection zone increases, as the aircraft gets closer to the airport runway.

Explain the terrain/obstacle awareness alerting and display database.

During all phases of fight, the EGPWS is predicting potential conflicts with terrain or obstacles in the flight path of the aircraft. The database includes all known obstacles higher than 100 feet AGL. The computer looks at flight path, ground speed and vertical speed to generate warnings of possible conflicts.

What MFD formats will allow terrain information to be presented?

- FMS map

- Nav sector

Does the terrain function of the EGPWS have to be displayed on the MFD to be active?

No, it is active at all times.

Can weather and terrain be displayed at the same time on the MFD?

No

How is the weather and terrain displayed on the MFD?

By pressing the WX/TERR button on the display control panel (DCP).

When is the terrain function active?

It is active all the time but it may not be displayed at all times.

What happens when conflicting obstacles or terrain are detected and the terrain feature is not displayed on the MFD?

The MFD range is automatically set to 10 miles and the terrain overlay is displayed. The pilots will hear "CAUTION TERRAIN or CAUTION OBSTACLE" over the speaker. The amber GRD PROX glare shield switch light will flash.

What will happen to the radar display when a terrain/obstacle alert occurs?

The radar display on the MFD will be replaced by the terrain display. The RADAR in the top left corner of the MFD display is replaced with TERRAIN.

Can the EGPWS terrain be inhibited?

Yes, on the GRD PROX panel there is a terrain OFF switch light.

Explain the excessive descent rate mode 1 of the EGPWS.

This mode starts at 2,500 feet AGL using the radio altimeter. If the outer boundary is penetrated it will activate an aural "SINK RATE" and the yellow flashing EGPWS glare shield switch light. This boundary is desensitized if the aircraft is capturing the glide slope from above or recapturing the localizer from above.

If the inner boundary is entered, this will activate the aural "WHOOP WHOOP, PULL UP" and the red flashing EGPWS switch light on the glare shield. The aural warning will continue until the descent rate is corrected.

Explain EGPWS mode 2: excessive terrain closure rate.

If the aircraft is approaching terrain at an excessive rate, an alert will be generated. To generate this alert, the EGPWS uses the radio altimeter, vertical speed and the EGPWS databases. The aircraft can be in level flight or descending.

The two sub-modes for mode 2 are mode 2A and mode 2B.

- Mode 2A will first generate a "TERRAIN TERRAIN" aural message with the yellow GRND PROX switch light illumination. Once the "Pull Up" envelope is entered, the aural "WHOOP WHOOP PULL UP" will sound until the envelope is exited. When the warning envelope is exited, the aural "TERRAIN TERRAIN" and yellow GRND PROX switch light will continue until a 300 feet altitude gain or 45 seconds, or the 2,500 feet ability of the radio altimeter is exceeded.

- Mode 2B is used during normal approaches and landing. This mode is enabled when: 1. Flaps are in landing configuration, 2. ILS approach and the aircraft is +/- 2 dots of both LOC and GS and 3. The first 60 seconds after takeoff. If the aircraft enters the envelope with either the gear or flaps not in landing configuration, the warnings are the same as in mode 2A. If the mode 2A envelope is entered with the gear and flaps in landing configuration, the aural "TERRAIN TERRAIN" and GRND PROX switch light will warn the pilots until the envelope is exited.

Explain EGPWS Mode 3, altitude loss after takeoff.

This mode will generate a "DON'T SINK" aural and the yellow GRND PROX glare shield light will flash and will remain on until a positive rate of climb is established. These alerts will occur during takeoff or go around when the altitude loss permitted by the computer is exceeded. This altitude loss is based on the height of the aircraft above the ground.

This mode is active during takeoff or a missed approach when the landing gear is up and the flaps are not in the landing position. When the aircraft has gained sufficient altitude or is not in the takeoff or missed approach mode, mode 3 is no longer enabled.

Explain the EGPWS mode 4 unsafe terrain clearance.

This mode uses information from the radio altimeter and compares the aircrafts position with the EGPWS database. The alerts are provided during climb out, cruise, descent and approach for insufficient terrain clearance. There are 3 sub modes for mode 4:

- Mode 4A: This mode keeps you from landing gear up by having a "TOO LOW GEAR" envelope. It also provides protection from terrain where the terrain does not rise significantly or the aircrafts descent rate is not excessive. The standard boundary begins at 500 feet AGL and up to 190 KIAS with the gear retracted; this will generate a "TOO LOW GEAR" and yellow glare shield light. As the airspeed increases above 190 KIAS, the envelope increases to 1,000 feet AGL and this will generate a "TOO LOW TERRAIN" aural with the yellow glare shield lights.

- Mode 4B: This mode keeps you form landing with the flaps in a position other than landing configuration with the gear down. The envelope begins at 1,000 feet AGL on the radio altimeter. A "TOO LOW TERRAIN" aural will first be generated with the yellow glare shield lights. If the speed is less than 159 knots at 245 feet AGL, a "TOO LOW FLAP" aural with the yellow glare shield lights is generated. The FLAP OVRD switch can be used to silence this warning if landing at other than flaps 45 degrees is needed.

- Mode 4C: This mode is active on take off or go-around with the gear and flaps not in landing configuration. The envelope increases with altitude gain. This mode is used when the terrain is rising faster than the aircraft is climbing. The alert will be "TOO LOW TERRAIN" aural with the yellow glare shield lights.

Explain EGPWS mode 5: below glide slope deviation alert.

There are basically two types of alerts when the aircraft deviates below the glide slope. The first occurs at 1.3 dots below the glide slope and is called a "soft" alert because the aural "GLIDESLOPE" is less than the second alert. The yellow glare shield lights will flash with the alert.

The second alert occurs at 300 feet AGL at more than 2 dots below the glide slope. This is the hard alert and is louder than the first alert. If either deviation increases, the repetition aural rate and glare shield lights will increase.

Can the EGPWS glide slope deviation alert be cancelled?

If either glide slope switch light is pressed when the aircraft is below 1000 feet AGL, this will inhibit mode 5, below glide slope mode.

What radio altitudes are wind shear conditions monitored by the EGPWS?

10 to 1500 feet AGL

Explain an EGPWS wind shear alert.

A wind shear alert occurs when there are increasing performance conditions. This is a headwind or updraft. When these conditions exist, an amber pitch limit indicator (Alpha Margin Indicator, AMI) and an amber WINDSHEAR will appear on the PFD. The FDs will only provide escape guidance when the TOGA button is pressed, and it only provides GA pitch of 10 degrees. There will be a wind shear mode displayed in the FMA.

Explain an EGPWS wind shear warning.

This alert occurs when there is a tailwind or downdraft, which causes decreasing performance. There will be an aural "WINDSHEAR WINDSHEAR WINDSHEAR", a red WINDSHEAR and the AMI on the PFD. The FD's will provide escape guidance immediately up to 15 degrees. The FMA will indicate wind shear mode.

Two seccnds after the wind shear warning the autopilot will automatically disconnect. If the autopilot is engaged during these two seconds it will follow the FDs.

This alert has priority over all other warnings.

Which escape guidance, the FD or the AMI should be followed during a wind shear warning?

Follow the FD and if it appears that ground contact is going to occur, pitch for the AMI.

What is the TCAS monitoring range?

40 NM

What are the four TCAS display threat levels and display icons?

- Other traffic: This is any traffic within the 40 NM range and is indicated by an open cyan diamond.

- Proximate traffic: Any traffic within 6 NM +/- 1200 and is indicated by a solid diamond.

- Traffic Advisory (TA): Conflicting aircraft is 40 seconds from crossing paths and is indicated by a yellow solid circle.

- Resolution Advisory (RA): Conflicting aircraft is 25 seconds from crossing paths and is indicated by a red box.

When will the up or down arrow appear on a TCAS aircraft symbol?

When the TCAS aircraft is climbing or descending at 500 fpm or greater.

Which advisories have aural alerts?

Traffic advisory and resolution advisory have aural alerts.

What advisories are given to the pilots for a traffic advisory?

- Above the VSI amber TRAFFIC is displayed.

- The traffic is displayed on the PFDs as a solid amber circle.

- There is an aural "TRAFFIC TRAFFIC".

What are the two types of resolution advisories (RA)?

- Preventive RA - the RA will tell the pilot not to fly in a certain vertical direction.

- Corrective RA - the RA will tell the pilot to change the current vertical flight path.

The RA instructions will also be displayed on the PFD VSI.

How soon must the pilot initiate an RA escape maneuver?

The pilot must react within 2.5 seconds.

What happens if the TCAS determines the corrective action is not enough?

The tone of the aural alert increases in urgency. The TCAS will tell the pilot to increase climb or descent.

What is the minimum climb rate for an aural TCAS RA "CLIMB, CLIMB, CLIMB"?

The minimum is 1500 fpm (same for "DESCENT, DESCEND, DESCEND").

What should the pilot do if an "INCREASE CLIMB" is heard?

Increase climb rate to a minimum of 2500 fpm. It is the same response for "INCREASE DESCENT".

During a TCAS RA what will indicate the correct VSI to maintain?

The green arc on the VSI.

While on an ILS, just pass the FAF you receive an RA "CLIMB, CLIMB, CLIMB", what would you do?

Execute a go around immediately responding to the RA. Make sure to configure the aircraft.

While on an ILS just pass the FAF at 1300 feet AGL, is it possible to receive a descending RA?

Yes, but at 1000 feet AGL and below the descend RA is inhibited.

When are all RAs inhibited?

- Descending: Below 900 feet AGL

- Climbing: Below 1100 feet AGL

While climbing just after takeoff passing 1300 feet AGL, is it possible to receive a descending RA?

Yes, descending RAs are inhibited below 1200 feet AGL while climbing. Below 1200 feet AGL you need to think for yourself.

What are the three modes of the TCAS on the main page?

- STBY: All TCAS interrogations are inhibited.

- AUTO: TAs and RAs will be provided.

- TA ONLY: Only traffic advisories will be provided.

Explain the difference between REL and ABS on the TCAS main page.

- ABS displays the barometric altitude of the target aircraft.

- REL displays the altitude difference between the target aircraft and your aircraft.

Explain the TCAS test.

The test key selection is on the TCAS main page on the RTU. When selected the following will occur:

- Above the VSI will be TCAS TEST.

- The VSI scale will display an RA.

- If TCAS is selected on the MFD, the four different TCAS symbols will appear.

- There will be an aural "TCAS SYSTEM TEST OK" or "TCAS SYSTEM TEST FAIL" at the end of the test.

Explain the Other Traffic Key on the TCAS main page.

If OFF the non-threat traffic up to 40 NM will not be displayed. These are the open diamonds.

Explain the ABOVE, NORM and BELOW selections on the TCAS main page.

- NORM: The range of surveillance is 2700 feet above and below the aircraft.

- ABOVE: The range is 9900 feet above and 2700 feet below.

- BELOW: The range is 9900 feet below and 2700 feet above.

- If ABOVE and BELOW are selected the altitude range will be 9900 feet above and below.

How is the TCAS displayed on the MFD?

The TFC button on the DCP allows the TCAS to be displayed on the MFD. There will be little tick marks around the inner ring of the range marks of the MFD.

Does the OFF mode of the radar park the antenna?

Yes

Does the radar transmit during the test mode?

No

Explain the MAP mode of the radar?

Used to map the terrain. The path attenuation alerts (PAC) and the ground clutter suppression (GCS) are disabled.

Explain the GAIN control knob.

Gain is used to adjust the color of the radar picture. NORM is the position that gives the best presentation under most conditions. Each position away from NORM adjusts the color level by one. You can say it adjusts the sensitivity.

When the gain control is moved from NORM it should always be returned to NORM when finished. This is so you don't forget and you or someone else later interprets a cell incorrectly.

Explain what happens when the center of the GAIN knob (PUSH GCS) is pressed.

When the WX mode is active, the ground clutter suppression (GCS) decreases the intensity of the ground returns displayed on the radar. This allows the precipitation returns to be more accurately interpreted. The GCS will operate for 12 seconds after being activated. GCS will be displayed on the MFD radar mode line.

What is the degree range of the radar tilt?

+/-15 degrees

What is the beam width of the radar?

12 degrees

What tilt setting puts the bottom of the beam level with the horizon?

+6 degrees

Explain the auto-tilt button.

When selected, the auto-tilt feature automatically adjusts the beam for different altitudes and ranges to maintain the antenna tilt angle to the angle desired by the pilot. This is based on the previous selected tilt settings.

It reduces pilot workload by automatically readjusting the antenna tilt after a range or altitude change. When selected there will be an "A" next to the antenna tilt.

Explain the STAB radar button.

This turns on or off the stabilization function. When un-stabilized an amber USTB is displayed on the radar line. The stabilization automatically adjusts the radar to maintain the selected antenna tilt with the horizon as the aircraft turns and makes pitch changes.

Explain the SEC button on the radar.

The sector scan has to selections, +/- 60 and +/- 30 degrees. The SEC button is used to select between the two. SEC allows or a faster refresh rate.

Explain the XFR button on the radar control panel.

This button determines which pilot has control of the radar range with the standard installation. The pilot who has control will have range markers that are white and the pilot without control will have amber. If the non-controlling pilot has their range at something that does not match the controlling pilots, they will have a message RADAR NOT AT THIS RANGE on their MFD. They will have to select the same range to have a radar display.

The captain lost control of the radar range on his MFD, what would you do?

Select the XFR button on the radar control panel and let the FO change the radar range.

What two MFD formats allow the radar to be overlaid?

- NAV SECTOR

- FMS MAP

Explain the path attenuation correction and alert (PAC).

When an area of weather absorbs a significant amount of the radar energy, the radar sensitivity is corrected to give an accurate image. If the cell of weather uses the full correction ability of the radar, a PAC Alert will be given. A PAC Alert is given by displaying a yellow arc at the top of the radar display. This is an area with a shadow and should be avoided.

chapter 18

Oxygen

What is the source of supplemental oxygen for the flight deck?

An oxygen cylinder supplies the three oxygen masks on the fight deck.

Where is the flight deck oxygen bottle located?

The bottle is located under the cabin floor near the front right.

What are the three modes of the flight deck oxygen masks?

- Normal diluted demand: ambient air is mixed with the oxygen.

- 100% pure oxygen.

- 100% continuous flow under pressure.

What is the fully charged pressure of the flight deck oxygen bottle?

1850 PSI

Where are the oxygen pressure indications located?

It is displayed on the EICAS and also on the oxygen services panel outside. This is the small panel on the right front of the aircraft.

At what PSI will the crew be alerted of an oxygen low pressure?

At 1410 PSI the EICAS will display an amber OXY LO PRESS on ED1. The oxygen PSI reading on ED 2 will turn amber.

How would you know if you have enough oxygen pressure for a flight with a jump-seater?

Use the chart to check based on outside temperature. It is probably in your POH.

How would you know if the oxygen bottle had an overpressure condition?

The EICAS PSI reading would be an amber 0 with an amber OXY LO PRESS amber EICAS message. The green oxygen discharge indicator on the forward right side of the aircraft would of blown out.

Where is the oxygen service panel located?

The right side of the forward fuselage.

Explain how to test the crew oxygen mask.

Press the TEST button on the oxygen mask container and hold it during the complete test. This will cause the flow blinker to display a yellow cross and then disappear, which indicates that oxygen is flowing. Then squeeze the red release levers; this will cause the harness to inflate. Press the emergency flow control knob to check if continuous flow is available. Make sure the emergency flow control knob is in 100%.

Explain the white ON flag located in the door of the crew oxygen mask container.

When the mask is out of the container and in use, a white ON flag is in view on the left door. This indicates the oxygen shutoff valve is open.

What position should the NORMAL 100% lever be in at all times when the mask is not in use?

It should be in the 100% position. When the mask is needed, the situation can be assessed and if the N (normal) position for diluted oxygen can be used, then the pilot can select it.

How is the crew oxygen supply pressure adjusted on the mask?

The emergency flow control knob adjusts the pressure. The knob is rotated to adjust the supply pressure. EMERGENCY provides constant flow of oxygen at a low positive pressure.

How could you purge the crew oxygen mask of smoke?

Press the emergency flow control knob momentarily on the mask. This will provide a burst of positive air pressure.

How is the crew oxygen mask microphone selected?

By the MASK/BOOM switch on the ACP associated with that mask.

At high altitudes can the oxygen be diluted with ambient air?

When the cabin altitude reaches 30,000 feet, the flow will be 100% oxygen in either NORMAL or 100%.

How many passenger masks are on each side of the cabin?

Three on the first officer's side and two on the captain's side of the aircraft.

How are the passenger oxygen masks manually deployed?

Pressing the PASS OXY switch light on the flight deck normally deploys the masks. The flight attendant can use a pin (special pin, safety pin, etc.) to manually deploy each individual mask.

When the PASS OXY switch light on the flight deck is illuminated, does that mean the passenger masks have deployed?

It means that the signal has been sent to drop the masks but they may not of dropped.

How many times can an oxygen generator be used?

The oxygen generator can be used one time.

What starts the flow of oxygen to the passenger masks?

When the passenger pulls the mask down, the lanyard is pulled and starts the chemical reaction, which provides the oxygen.

Besides above the passenger seats, are there any other passenger oxygen masks in the cabin?

There is one passenger oxygen mask located in the lavatory and the flight attendant has one above the jump seat.

Why should a person not touch the oxygen generator?

The generator can reach temperatures of 500 F (260 C) when in use.

The flight attendant calls up during the use of passenger oxygen and tells you she smells a burning odor coming from the oxygen generators, is this an indication of a problem?

The generators may create a burning smell and this is normal.

What controls the automatic dropping of the passenger masks?

The cabin pressurization acquisition module (CPAM) controls the automatic deployment of the passenger oxygen masks. When the CPAM detects a cabin altitude of 14,000 feet, it sends an electrical signal to the containers to release the masks.

What are the components of the portable oxygen system?

- Protective breathing equipment (PBE)
- Portable oxygen cylinder
- Portable mask

What are the locations of the PBEs?

Usually one on the flight deck, one at the flight attendant area and one in the aft of the cabin.

What emergency equipment is located on the flight deck? (Your aircraft may be different)

- Three oxygen masks
- PBE
- Oxygen bottle
- Escape rope
- Escape hatch
- Crash ax
- Three life vests
- Flare gun
- Two flash lights
- Fire extinguisher

What emergency equipment is located in the cabin (your aircraft may be different)?

Forward entrance compartment:

- PA/Interphone.

- 1 Life vest.

- 1 PBE.

- 1 Halon fire extinguisher.

- 1 Flashlight.

- 2 Portable oxygen bottles with masks.

- 1 First aid kit.

- 3 Infant flotation devices.

- Equipment for demos.

Other areas:

- Emergency medical kit, which may be at the front or the rear of the aircraft.

- Automatic external defibrillator (AED).

- 1 Water fire extinguisher.

- 2 Lifelines located at row 8.

- All seat cushions are flotation devices.

- Safety information cards.

What is the duration of the passenger oxygen once it is activated?

Duration of the oxygen is approximately 13 minutes.

When will the passenger oxygen masks automatically deploy?

The masks will automatically deploy when the CPAM detects a cabin altitude of 14,000 feet.

chapter 19

Pneumatic System

What are the sources of 10th stage air?

- Engines

- APU

- External air

When can the right side of the 10th stage manifold be pressurized by any source?

When the 10th stage isolation valve is open.

Where is the external ground air connector located?

The connection is just aft of the aft cargo door.

What is the purpose of the external ground air connector?

This connection is for external ground air to be supplied to the 10th stage for cooling of the cabin or engine starting.

Where are the left and right 10th stage bleed shut-off valves (SOV) located?

They are located in the aft equipment bay.

How are the 10th stage bleed SOVs operated?

The valves are pneumatically operated and electrically controlled. It takes air pressure and electrical power for the valves to open.

What happens to the 10th stage bleed air valves if electrical power or pneumatic air is lost?

The valves are spring-loaded closed.

During what system problems will the 10th stage bleed air valves close automatically?

When a system over-pressure or over-temperature is detected.

What does the pilot do to open the 10th stage bleed air valves during engine starts?

The opening of these valves is automatic during engine starts.

What is the purpose of the 10th stage isolation valve?

The valve is used to isolate the left and right sides of the 10th stage bleed air manifold. When opened it allows both sides of the 10th stage manifold to be fed by one source of 10th stage bleed air.

Is DC or AC power needed to open the 10th stage isolation valve?

DC power

Explain the APU load control valve interlock protection.

Located in the APU bleed air duct is a check valve which prevents 10th stage bleed air from flowing back to the APU. This is the first level of protection to the APU compressor. If high-pressure air from the engines was allowed to flow back to the APU, damage could result. The second level of protection is the interlock protection of the APU LCV.

If the left 10th stage SOV is selected open with the APU LCV open, the APU LCV would close automatically. If the APU LCV is open and the right

10th stage SOV is selected open with the ISOL valve open the APU LCV would automatically close. This all commanded by the switch position of the 10th stage SOVs and not the valve position.

What triggers the APU LCV closure when the 10th stage bleed air valve is open and the APU LCV is open?

The 10th stage bleed air switch position, not the flow of 10th stage air from the engines or SOV position. The APU electronic control unit ECU) monitors these switch positions.

With the APU LCV open, will opening the right 10th stage bleed air valve cause the APU LCV to close?

Only if the 10th stage ISOL valve is also selected open.

What uses 14th stage bleed air to operate?

- Thrust reversers.

- Anti-icing of the wing leading edge and engine cowl.

How is reverse flow of 14th stage bleed air from engine to engine prevented?

Check valves prevent reverse flow.

How is the 14th stage bleed air SOVs operated?

The SOVs are pneumatically operated and electrically controlled. It takes air pressure and electrical power to operate the SOVs.

What position will the 14th stage bleed air SOVs fail?

Open

What position will the 14th stage isolation valve fail?

Closed

What must be on for the 14th stage isolation valve to operate?

The 14th stage bleed valves must be open to begin with. The wing anti-ice must be on for the 14th stage isolation valve to operate. This is due to the isolation valve being down stream of the wing anti-ice valves and needing pneumatic pressure to operate.

What areas does the bleed air leak detection system monitor?

The system monitors the wing areas, the fuselage and the pylon.

How many overheat detection loops does the 10th and 14th stage have?

- 10th stage: Dual loop

- 14th stage: Single loop

How is the wing anti-ice system monitored for overheat conditions?

The fuselage uses a single loop overheat detection and thermal switches in the leading edges of the wings.

At what point in the wing anti ice system does the wing overheat system provide monitoring?

Monitoring begins at the wing anti-ice valves to through the wing.

What is the benefit to the design of dual overheat detection loops?

Both loops must detect the overheat condition, which minimizes false warnings. If one loop fails, the aircraft can still be dispatched with a single detection loop operating.

Explain how a bleed air leak is directed onto the detection loops.

An outer cover that has holes at certain points encases the ducts. The sensing loops are installed next to these holes, which will direct the heat onto the sensing loops.

What do the wing leading edges use to detect an overheat condition?

Thermal switches detect overheat conditions.

Explain the test positions of the DUCT MON knob on the bleed air control panel.

- TEST: This test simulates an overheat and logic test of the 10th and 14th stage bleed air leak detection systems.

- LOOP A or B: Tests for short circuits in the 10th stage dual loops.

TEST: Simulates an overheat condition in the 10th and 14th stage manifolds and the wing anti ice duct. The 10th and 14th DUCT FAIL lights on the bleed air panel and the DUCT FAIL in the WING TEST switch light illuminates.

Five EICAS warning messages appear on the EICAS, R & L 14th DUCT, R & L 10th DUCT, ANTI ICE DUCT. There will also me a green DUCT TEST OK on ED2.

Loop A and B: These positions will illuminate a STATUS message DUCT MON LOOP A or B.

What do the DUCT FAIL lights in the L or R 10th stage bleed switch lights indicate?

There is a bleed air leak in the associated duct. It means it is doing its job of detecting a bleed air leak. The switch lights will also illuminate during the TEST position of the DUCT MON switch.

What is the meaning of an illuminated FAIL light in the APU LCV switch light?

The LCV is open when the interlock protection has commanded it closed.

When the glare shield Fire Push Switch is pressed, what bleed valves close?

The 10th and 14th stage SOVs close.

What do the DUCT FAIL lights in the14th stage bleed switch lights indicate?

There is a bleed air leak in the associated duct.

chapter 20

Water & Waste

Do the galley and lavatory sink share the same potable water supply?

There are two separate water systems but almost identical. The galley water container is located under the galley floor and the lavatory water container is in the upper fuselage area of the cargo compartment.

Where are the controls for the water systems?

The controls for both systems are located on a control panel located in the galley.

Are the galley and lavatory tanks heated?

The galley tank heater prevents the water from freezing and the lavatory tank heater is used to warm the water for delivery to the sink. These controls are located at the flight attendants station.

The hoses to the galley and lavatory are heated along with the overboard masts and drain lines

What other areas of the water system is heated?

The drain lines, masts and hose assemblies are heated.

CRJ Aircraft Systems Study Guide

How are the water tanks refilled?

There are two service points, one in the front and one in the rear of the aircraft on the right side.

How are the heaters to the drain masts, line heaters and water system activated?

The control switches on the control panel in the galley.

Where is the location of the service panel for the waste disposal system?

An access panel is located at the right rear of the fuselage.

Where is the indication for the water level of the toilet located?

There is no indication.

Sources

Bombardier Inc. Canadair Regional Jet Pilot Reference Manual

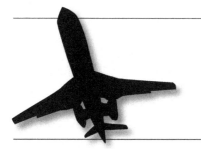

Author Biography

Aaron Boone has his ATP, CFI, CFII and MEI certificates. He is type rated in the Canadair Regional Jet - CRJ200, Embraer Brasilia - EMB120, Citation CE-500, CE-560XL and the King Air BE-300. He was an airline captain for a large regional airline and has previously been a flight instructor, freight pilot and corporate pilot.

With a BA in Psychology he understands what it takes to get ready for a checkride and to keep your CRJ knowledge in top shape. Aaron used his study system through college to greatly improve the efficiency of his study time and easily made good grades. He then carried this study system into aviation with very good success in training.

Made in the USA
Middletown, DE
07 November 2019